IT'S ALL ABOUT ENERGY

A Beginner's Guide to Accessing
Your Energetic SUPERPOWER
Physically, Personally, and Professionally

CARI MOFFET

BIG MOOSE
PUBLISHING

DEDICATION

To the thousands of bodies I have had the privilege and honour of working with throughout my career.

To my husband, Craig, because you drive me nuts and I love you. You are seriously one of my greatest teachers.

To my cats, Wrigley and Fenway, because no one dedicates books to cats and I want to be the first!

CONTENTS

ACKNOWLEDGMENTS

I am extremely grateful for the people who have come into my life to teach me more about who I am and why I'm here. Sometimes we think people are assholes, or idiots, when really they are mirrors of what more we can be. I will not list the assholes, because they already know who they are!

I am thankful for my family. We may not agree on many philosophies of life, but we still love and are able to accept each other for where we are at. That is the greatest gift of all. Mom, Dad, sister Jodi and family, grandparents, and in-laws – thank you!

Friends, colleagues, and acquaintances, life is more colourful with you! There are too many to list. If we have said hello, this is YOU.

I am thankful to the teachers in my life. Fay Thompson, Glenyce Hughes, Caroline Stewart, Bonnie Wirth, Abe Brown, Brenda Nightengale, Leonie Dawson, Bonnie Bogner, Fatima Shariff, and Tillie Dyck, you have impacted me more than you will ever know. For any others I have missed, thank you for appearing and living your greatest truth in teaching. It takes balls to share and to be yourself.

Lastly, thank you to the people who can put shit together on paper better than I can. I have many qualities, but grammar and spelling are not amongst them. Thanks to hubby Craig, Maggie Stock, and Fay at Big Moose Publishing.

INTRODUCTION

I didn't know there was a book inside of me. It was one chilly day in the winter of 2019 when an ad from Leonie Dawson came across my computer to "Write a Book in 40 Days". I was familiar with Leonie's work, because I had purchased a couple of her business day planners in the past. She is a hard working mom from Australia who has the most humorous and artistic way of communicating. Knowing I had 40 days of staying indoors with our lovely Canadian weather, I accepted the challenge and the birthing process of this book began.

It's amazing how many self-doubt and self-mutilating thoughts go along with this process. *Will anyone even be interested in this information?* *"Everyone knows this stuff."* *"What am I doing? I can't write a book."* But, Leonie kept encouraging me. She opened my mind to new chapters. Then, all of a sudden, my baby (this book) was born.

The following pages hold a lot of my life's experience and

the lessons I have learned. Recognizing that it's all about energy and learning to work with it has been the greatest asset to my life. You will read about my two husbands (no, I'm not a polygamist – just one at a time), and about how I have no children by choice (and finally now in my 40's people have stopped asking if I will have kids). You will see my career progression as a Registered Massage Therapist, Energy Healer, and Medical Intuitive. This is really where the world of Energy Medicine began to appear in my life. You will also read about some of my client's experiences (all with permission), and there are a few unbelievable accounts in working with the body and others' energy. I really love all that I do as far as a career, and know this is why I am here – to shine a light for people who are looking for that too. Our lights shine brighter when we find more of who we are. Then, all of a sudden, we realize we are not alone and no longer need to label ourselves a freak.

Join me in this journey and you will probably find yourself in these words. I will show you easy ways to work with your own energy through some thought provoking questions found at the end of each chapter. Pour some wine and grab a journal. Jot down your thoughts or just write in this book (it's your book; I give you permission). Feel free to read this book cover to cover or one section at a time. There is no wrong. Thank you for picking this book up, and if you enjoy it, let others know who would too. Share away!

YOU **SERIOUSLY** ARE ENERGY:

The body is made up of systems and organs.

Systems and organs are made up of tissue.

Tissue is made up of cells.

Cells are made up of molecules.

Molecules are made up of atoms.

Atoms are made up of subatomic particles.

Subatomic particles are made up of energy.

PART 1

THE ENERGY OF LIFE

*When you are evolving into a higher self, the road
may seem lonely, but you're simply shedding the
energies that no longer match the frequency of your
destiny.*

~ Unknown

CHAPTER 1

SHINE YOUR LIGHT

It was 2004 when my new husband, Craig, convinced me we should sell everything we own and move from Canada to England. I resisted this idea at first, but then thought, "When am I ever going to have an opportunity to do this?"

Still unsure if this was a good move, Craig took me to London for a week to see if we would both enjoy it. After three theatre productions, one castle, and a couple fish and chips meals, I was sold. Within the year we said goodbye to everyone we loved and everything we owned, and off we went to start a life in Sutton, Surrey, England.

It felt like a holiday for the first few months. Everything

was new and different. England made our history books come alive as we saw things that we had only ever read about. We travelled around Europe every chance we could, and, even to this day, that may just be the best part of the entire experience.

During our time in England, I found a massage therapist named Fatima that I saw regularly. One day she asked me what was wrong since I looked a bit haggard. I confessed that the chiropractic practice that we leased was a constant struggle, I was severely homesick which I never knew was a real thing until this adventure, and my legs from my knees down were out of this world itchy.

The mysterious itch was actually my first concern. It was the most frustrating feeling. I could go to the doctor, but from knowing my body, I knew it wasn't a lack of corticosteroid cream that was the problem. I just didn't know the answer.

After hearing my struggles, Fatima asked if she could do some Reiki on me. My first thought was "Reiki is so evil." After thinking this, I realized that wasn't my own thought. That is what my family believed. With them being 3000 miles away, it suddenly didn't matter.

Reluctantly I agreed to the Reiki treatment, really having no clue what it was. Fatima did a bit of massage and then a bit of energy work. She placed her hands on me in such a gentle way that it made me wonder why people think this is so evil. All at the same time, I was praying that if this was evil, for God to counteract what was happening. (I am seriously laughing behind my computer right now.) I honestly felt nothing with what she did, but it was what she said that made me curious as to what this mysterious evil energy work really could be. She read the energy of my body, interpreted it, and then relayed this message:

"Cari, your body wants you to either plant your roots in England or take yourself back to your home country. It feels like your energy body is still in Canada. It is not feeling grounded or planted in your actual physical place. You have a choice. We always have a choice!"

That was a crazy message for me; yet, it resonated so deeply. I knew I didn't want to plant roots in England. I mentioned it to my husband and suggested that we should move back to Canada. He actually didn't fight it too hard even though our original plan was to stay for ten years. We would be leaving after two.

We started making plans to return to Canada. We quit our practice, booked our flights, and before we knew it, we were travelling home. The funny thing is that I have not had that itch on my legs since landing back in my home country!

Before I left England, I learned levels one and two Usui Reiki from Fatima. She was such an angel of inspiration to me. I have lost touch with her, but if she ever finds this book, I hope she contacts me. Since Fatima's teachings, I have finished the Reiki Master Program and have helped many learn Reiki by teaching classes. I have worked on thousands with this energy modality to encourage balance of the body, mind, and spirit. The ripple effect has been huge, and all from my itchy legs!

I've wondered from time to time how this life would have played out if Fatima wasn't brave enough to suggest Reiki and deliver this message. I have also wondered how different my life would have been if I had not listened to my own intuition, but rather followed the beliefs from my upbringing.

We came back to Canada and chose to put our roots down in my hometown (a place I vowed to never return). It's funny how things always happen for a reason. After being gone for 15 years, it wasn't easy to return home. I had learned so much about energy that I was now passionate about. Still many people viewed my energy work as evil and judged me as wrong for practicing it.

One day, one of my own family members picked up my Reiki magazine and laughed at it saying, "You don't believe in this stuff, do you?" I was a bit stunned and didn't say anything, even though I was preparing to teach my very first Reiki class. A similar experience came from my massage therapy practice. When a massage client saw my Reiki certificate on my wall, she became scared that I was going to do Reiki on her, and made a point of telling me she would have none of that.

On a different occasion, one lady was quite upset that I

was practicing Reiki in our town. She literally threw a bible at me and told me that what I was doing was not from God. I have had professionals not want to work with me because of what I practice and what I believe. I have been treated differently by people who I used to socialize with, all because I adopted a different belief because of my life experience (because of my damn itchy legs!)

I share these stories because this is usually how people act when they are afraid of something new. None of them would be able to tell you what Reiki is; yet, they believe no one should do it because it is evil. Where does this evil come from? Judgment is pretty evil, too.

This is why, I believe, many healers hide. Judgment hurts and it's almost easier to stay in the shadows than put yourself out there. I felt this deeply with my move back to small town Saskatchewan. I wasn't alone though. I just needed to find my peeps!

I continued with my massage practice and was likely the only professional advertising Reiki services at the time. I kept running across others who knew Reiki or some other energy modality. I decided to invite them to a gathering in my little massage room so that I could get to know them. To my surprise, 13 people showed up! I felt like we were having an underground meeting (and I guess we sort of were) in a town that they, too, felt the judgment for being different.

The year was 2006 and I felt I had met my tribe. This began a whole new journey of practice in my small conservative town. I believe by meeting each other we strengthened one another. We started shining our lights as bright as we possibly could. (That is what we were born to do now, isn't it?) There is no benefit to anyone when that light is covered and hidden. It's time to shine. It's time to be brave and vulnerable. It's time to change this world!

Thoughts to Ponder:

1. Where are you experiencing body symptoms that are mysterious and needing an interpreter to relay messages?
2. Are there things in your life that you are resisting because of fear?
3. Are there people in your life who you have let dim your light?
4. Who is in your tribe that supports your shining light?

CHAPTER 2

EVERYONE IS A TEACHER AND EVERYONE IS A STUDENT

When I was little, I wanted to be a teacher. In fact, I would make my friends play school after class. (Sorry Coral and Rochelle.) This was quite ironic since I didn't really like school. Still, there was just some mysterious draw to being a teacher. As I grew older, this thought never crossed my mind again. Now, as an adult in my forties, I have stepped into the role of teacher many times, even in a private college setting.

Teaching what I have learned through life experience is exhilarating for me. I ponder events and people with curiosity and can find myself learning through most things, which makes me even more of a student than a teacher.

The vast majority of information in this book (and in most books) is not new information. It is recycled down from many thoughts and from many people. We are attracted to people who speak the same language and vibrate the same as us. Therefore, we can understand what they are saying even if it has been presented a million different times in a million different ways. We will only understand it when it resonates with our energy.

One example of this in my own life is with the author Eckhart Tolle and his book <u>The Power of Now</u>. I believe it was Oprah Winfrey who made Tolle more well-known by advertising his work on her show. Likely it was at that same time that I bought his book. I resonated with Oprah and watched the Oprah Winfrey Show almost every day. I listened closely when she said to buy Eckhart's book. "She is Oprah and it must be good," I thought.

When I opened up Tolle's book, I could barely read the introduction. It was so spiritually thick with new ways of thinking that I closed it up and put it back on my shelf for about 15 years. I kept it, because I didn't have the heart to give away a book I never really cracked. A few summers ago, I opened the book again and started devouring it! I loved it. It's a book that needs to be read over and over, because it contains so many concepts to practice in our lives.

Why didn't I resonate with the book 15 years earlier? Our vibrations were not the same. I realized this is important when I am finding teachers to guide me on my own journey. One thing I needed to keep in mind is that we are always changing and, therefore, so are our teachers.

I have had many great teachers in my life, and even some not so great who had hidden agendas and were not practicing what they preached. Once such mentor in my life hurt my soul deeply. I believed in the lessons she was teaching and I loved what was being said.

As time passed though, I realized the actions of her teachings were not measuring up. I discovered lies and dishonesty everywhere. The funny thing in my world was that others were seeing this far sooner than I was. Why was I still resonating with her teachings? Why did I still believe in her when others did not? This, too, is an example of resonation. One day I woke up vibrating so differently that the only choice I had was to get away from the situation, quit, and move on. If you ever come across a teacher who claims to know everything and their way is the only way – RUN! Run like Forrest Gump and don't look back.

In saying all of the above, I feel it's appropriate to thank the teachers who have influenced my life. Some of them I have never met. Some are still in my life and showing me more of how I want to live. Others have faded away, and I send them off with gratitude for what I have learned.

You may think that a teacher is someone who has taught a class or written a book. Not true. Everyone and everything can be a teacher for you and may hold messages significant to your life. We sometimes get in the way of needing to be right, and therefore miss the lesson the person is delivering.

The teachings any relationship delivers should be held without judgment. Even if you don't particularly like the person, they may have a life-changing lesson for you to pivot your beliefs. Relationships may end and give us a chance to examine ourselves and what we need or don't need, and what we want or don't want.

One of my greatest teachings that I am still learning is to allow others to be who they are. That's it! I do not have to judge them for their actions or speech. They are just being who they are. Most of us are living the best lives that we know how. If I judge them for being wrong, which is really saying 'you are different than me', then how much allowance will flow into and around my own life? Not much.

The vibration of judgment will actually attract more of the same and I will feel judged all the time, because I am judging. What if I allowed others to just be who they are? Would this not allow me to be who I am as well? Isn't that what we all want – the freedom to be who we are made to be, and then we can accomplish what we are meant to do?

Allowance means I don't have to change anyone, or fix anyone's 'mistakes', or get in the way of their life lessons. I just have to allow others to be themselves and allow myself to be me!

All of the stress we have with other people stems from our own expectations not being met. Think about someone you struggle with. What did they do or not do to create that struggle? Were you expecting something different, or something more or less from them? Likely! If we remove our own expectations on people and just allow them to be, do, and act the way they want, you too can have the freedom to be, do, and act the way you want. Removing the judgment from another's actions creates allowance for them and for you. If you didn't have people judging you or wanting you to meet their expectations, would you be doing something different with your life?

We are not done learning until our last breath. Some days in my massage therapy practice, I will be giving some homecare or intuitive insights to a client and stop myself and say, "This message is for me too." Like energy attracts like energy and daily I pay attention to what people are presenting physically, as well as emotionally in my practice, as there are many messages for me as well. We are like a mirror to our environment.

The most influential author through my life has been Carolyn Myss. In 1998, I went through what I call a live NDE (near death experience). Many people go through these with health or relationship breakups. Mine was a divorce at the age of 26 that prompted me to walk away from family expectations in regards to religion.

This time of life crushed my soul and turned me upside down. Myss' book, Anatomy of the Spirit, was like CPR to my spirit. I remember just being wowed and having many light bulb moments while reading it. We energetically resonated and I was definitely ready! I think I've read her book at least four times.

Truthfully, if I was not going through a messy relationship breakup, I would not have found her book. The vibrational resonance would not have connected us. Here's an even crazier truth: I would not be writing this book if I did not get divorced. This live NDE changed the direction of my life and gave me the greatest gift ever….ready for it….ME.

In the pages that follow, I will share with you lessons I have learned from those who have crossed my path. We can learn from both the roses and the thorns and the energy of the interactions. In each class that I teach, I have a saying that I would like you to adopt as you read: "Take what you can and discard the rest. Some may come back to you and some may not be meant for you. You decide. You are the teacher and you the student!"

Thoughts to Ponder:

1. Who has been and/or who is currently your teacher?
2. Who has influenced your life in a new direction? Have you brought gratitude to that relationship even if it was the hardest time of your life?
3. Have you practiced acceptance in all relationships with people who are different than you?
4. Are you continually learning from others and allowing for growth in your life?
5. Who is not meeting your expectations in life and why does it matter to you?

CHAPTER 3

YOUR FREQUENCY

What is energy really? You may have realized already that we hold vibrations within us. Here's a quote from Albert Einstein: "Everything is energy and that's all there is to it. Match the frequency of the reality you want and you cannot help but get that reality. It can be no other way."

Matching the frequency can be thought of as tuning into a radio station. You just need to find the station to be able to give you what you want: pop, country, classical, etc.

Many people talk about this in different ways. Let me lay out a very easy way to follow. Since you are energy, (because Einstein says everything is and that includes you) and you can change your vibration to high or low, then would you not have a superpower to create anything in life you desire? You have the power within you to achieve whatever it is you desire by finding the vibration of what is required. It's a big thought and one that can be life changing!

I never realized this vibrational power was within me until 2008 when I watched the unfolding of a dream that was nine years old. I built a wellness centre! This centre was dreamed up at a chiropractic seminar when the speaker asked a super cool question: "If time and money were of no concern, what would you be doing with your life?" I wrote down some boring answers about paying off my visa and student loans, but then she challenged us to go deeper and to really find that seed of joy that fires us up.

To be completely honest, I didn't even know this potential was within me. My thoughts on life at the time were to get a good job, have a family, and die. There was no dreaming in there! This was all I was shown from my family. Could I actually have more?

Eventually, I wrote that I would like to build a retreat centre. I then wrote out what it would look like and what it would offer. I tucked that away after the weekend was over and didn't really look at it with any form of seriousness. Still, it was there, and it had been acknowledged.

It took another eight years to remember this vision. One night at dinner with friends, the question came up as to what we would do if we won the lottery that night - a huge jackpot. When it was my turn to answer, I said, "I am not waiting to win a jackpot. I am going to build a wellness centre." I actually remember feeling shocked that it came out of my mouth. I was also a bit mad at myself, because I now had seven people who may hold me accountable. There was also the worry that this little statement might not come true.

I secretly hoped they didn't hear me, but then the questions started with what would it look like and what would it offer. I answered and they were supportive. This little seed was being watered!

There was the feeling inside of me of wonderment and excitement of how amazing this would be. This one question about the lottery started the vibration to find the proper radio station to set this dream in motion. The people around the table that night needed to hear my dream, because one of them was a Real Estate Agent who knew a great property that just came on the market under foreclosure. Another was a lawyer who helped seal the deal. I even had a friend that night that was in the linen business and ended up supplying all the linens for the massage therapists. I was, all of a sudden, the proud owner of a piece of property that was soon to become a wellness centre.

Once inside the building, I remember sitting there visualizing how to gut and rebuild the structure so that it would function efficiently as a wellness centre. Countless hours were spent thinking, drawing, visualizing, and vibrating to what this dream wanted to be. I could visualize people coming out of the rooms with that 'drunk after massage' look. I could see people hugging, people laughing, and people encouraging others to keep going through life. I could see it as a place of hope with the services we would offer as an alternative to western medicine. Every visualization came to reality including the structure of the office. Over the years this little dream grew and grew and we eventually had to renovate and expand to keep up to the demands.

Today's Wholelife Wellness is not the place that was originally thought of, either. The energy of the space changed and the business wanted to be something else. Many days and nights were filled with asking what it wanted to be, because the whole entity had its own energy with its own field and vibration. When you work with an entity that doesn't speak verbally, you must tune in intuitively to ask, "What now? What would you like to create and what would you like to be?" It is no different than asking yourself these questions. We will cover more about this in a later chapter.

The centre was a springboard for many providers to start

their own businesses. It was created as a seed to show others (mostly providers, but also clients) what is actually possible in their lives. Wholelife Wellness also invited the healers who were in their closets hiding to come out and play. It was now safe.

One of my favourite quotes is from Goethe. "Whatever you can do or dream you can, begin it. Boldness has genius, power, and magic in it." This makes sense to me now after experiencing this process first hand.

What are you wishing deep within you to create with your life? What do you want? This is one of the most important questions of your life! What do you want?

Countless people have bitched and complained on my massage table about how horrible their life is and when I ask these simple questions: "What do you want?", "What job would be fun for you?", or "Where would you like to live?", the most common answer is, "I don't know." Figure it out, because that is where the joy and magic of life is found! This is not just for a select few or the rich and powerful. It is for everyone, including you and me. There is no difference between us. This is the power that is available to us all. Is it worth spending some time going within, and asking for help?

Thoughts to Ponder:

1.   If time and money were of no concern, what would you be doing with your life?

2.   What do you really want while you are alive?

3.   Have you discovered the seed of joy that fires you up? Are you ready to grow it? What holds you back?

CHAPTER 4

CHANGE YOUR VIBE

One cannot understand energy without exploring vibrations. I remember being in Grade 5 (a very long time ago) and hearing our teacher say, "Everything is vibrating. Even this desk is vibrating!" I know I was laughing in my head thinking that the teacher was out to lunch, and that the desk was as solid as they came!

Today, I know that everything holds a vibration. There is an actual Theory of Vibration. (Feel free to google it if you are a need to know type of person!)

When I mentioned the Theory of Vibration to my mom one day, she had a bit of a chuckle and said she didn't believe in it. It is hard to believe in something we cannot see with our own eyes. She told me that in order to vibrate it must have life. I asked her what constituted something to be alive, and she said, "Blood." I think I literally said, "Is that your final answer?" Cheeky kid!

What about plants? Where is the blood? We undisputedly agree that a plant is alive. If everything holds a vibration, can we then say that everything is alive? Can we talk and ask a lamp stand questions and get answers? I may or may not have participated in an experiment to ask a lamp questions about a certain hotel. Do you know what the lamp said? "No one has ever asked me questions before." It did not speak vocally but both my friend and I picked that up intuitively. Now that you all think I'm crazy, I'll give you permission to take a break and go and talk to your furniture!

Dr. Masaru Emoto is an excellent example of showing the world how words hold different vibrations. In his book, The Hidden Messages in Water, he took molecules of water and exposed them for some time to different words such as love, hate, Hitler, peace, etc. He then took a photograph of each molecule of water. The photography is astonishing. Molecules that were exposed to words such as love or peace became beautiful crystals. Those exposed to words such as hate or kill looked sickly or malevolent. It makes one think even deeper about this vibrational bit. If water can hold a pattern of vibration with spoken word, what do our words do to us and others when our bodies are 70% water? This is a thought to seriously examine in your life.

Who and what do you surround yourself with? Think about the people you spend time with, the TV programs you watch, and the reading material you enjoy. What type of vibrations do they hold?

The box store Ikea did an experiment a few years ago involving two plants. One plant had a sign on it asking people to yell and shout their frustrations at it. The other plant had a sign asking people to show love and appreciation for it. Are you surprised when I say that the loved plant thrived and the other was quite droopy soon to be dead?

Even having this as an experiment is off-putting to some. How can one be so cruel to a plant? The same could be said for us. How can we be so cruel to ourselves with the words we use? Think about how we treat others around us - our partner, our children, our co-workers, or our extended family. All the words you have ever thought and said have held a vibration to droop or to thrive the other vibratory being it was intended for.

Don Miguel Ruiz, in his book <u>The Four Agreements,</u> states the first agreement is to be impeccable with your word. This is a statement that needs to be taken into serious consideration. When we see the power of just one word in Masaru Emoto's water experiments, how many words each day do we diminish our vibration with? How can we use our words to enhance our vibration and the vibration of others?

I have done an experiment of my own with this thought. Have you ever heard of witching wands to find water? I made wands out of a wire coat hanger. I cut off two sections about 8 inches long and bent them each at 90-degree angles. Then I took the ink out of 2 plastic pens and used them as holders for the wire so that the wires could move freely on their own without interference from me. I set the intention that these wands were to find the energy fields of people. (Yes, I talked to them and told them their job, and they listened just as well as the lamp!) When the field is found, my wands flare out so that the ends of the wire repel each other, similar to two magnets that have the same polarity.

One day, I decided to demonstrate this theory of energy fields and vibrations to an audience of teachers. After asking for a brave volunteer, we found the size of his normal field. It was about an arm's length away from his body. Then, I asked the volunteer to think of someone or something they dislike. There was a lot of laughter from the crowd as they watched. The field was tested again and I stood with the wands right up close to his nose.

Next, I asked the volunteer to think of something that he loved such as his kids or a pet. I tested his field again and the room was too small for his energy field. I then asked the audience to send the volunteer judgmental thoughts. I told the audience to pick the volunteer apart as though they were talking to themselves in a mirror. It was actually hard for most to do this (but, let's be honest, we all do this). Of course, after testing the volunteer, his energy field was small, right up to his skin. Then, we tested, as an entire group, sending love to the volunteer and the field was larger than the room. The last test I did was for us to send the volunteer judgment and have the volunteer project love. The result was that the field was just as large as the back walls of the 1000 square foot room.

Someone made an interesting point relating this experiment to group sports. Just imagine a child (or adult for that matter) messing up a basketball shot or letting in a goal. Likely the athlete projects frustration and maybe judgment towards himself or to the teammate who screwed up. It's not only that one person who is involved in the judgment. Think about the coach, the teammates, and the fans. If an athlete does not have the mindset to push out the other vibrations, they may be stuck in the lower vibes and keep screwing up for the team, often leading them to being pulled from the game. The energy of sports and life really are fascinating, and can be easily manipulated for our greater good.

Why does all this matter? When we have a smaller energy field around us, we tend to be more closed off and possibly defensive, because we are not occupying much space to include anything. You will likely become upset easily and become irritated by the slightest comments.

When our field is larger, we tend to be stronger mentally, physically, emotionally, and spiritually. More opportunities are attracted to a larger energy field. You will feel more powerful in your own space than when your field is small and restricted.

To keep a larger energy field, you can think about your kids and pets all day, but there are more ways to help sustain your energy. These include nutritious food, hydration, sunlight, laughter, music, and doing the things you love with those you love. All of these things contribute to a larger energy field, which will result in a higher vibration. With a higher vibe, you attract higher vibrations into your world. You are able to receive the bad and the ugly without your world crumbling. This doesn't mean you have to take on other people's stuff. It means that opportunities will come to you, because your high vibe antenna is up and signalling that you are in allowance of whatever comes your way. You can also handle situations with a response, instead of a strong reaction. Your ability to adapt and change will be greater.

Another way you can increase your vibrational energy field is to write out your 'Love List'. I suggest you attempt to write out 100 things that you absolutely love to do. Some people have gasped at this thought. Yes, you have at least 100 things that you love. You just may have forgotten some of them. These things can be as simple as sipping your favourite tea, watching movies, eating your favourite food, sitting around a campfire with friends, shopping, traveling, etc.

I challenge you to do at least 3 activities on your list per day. In a week, increase it to 5 per day. As time goes on, keep increasing it. You will find over time that you will begin to fill your day with things you love rather than with things that just occupy time or that you feel obligated to do. Why is this important? You will begin to incorporate more joy into your life. With more joy, your vibration is extraordinarily higher and your adaptability to life is greater. Change will not matter as much to you as it may to a lower vibrating person who will cling to lower vibrating habits when life throws a curve ball.

I suggest using your Love List forever. Pull out your list when you want to add more joy to your life or to just change up your vibration when you're having a lower vibrating day. We can all use help with our mental health and this is one way to keep us not only sane, but also happy.

Thoughts to Ponder:

1. Have you ever stopped to consider the vibration of the things around you?
2. How well do your pets, home, and houseplants vibrate? Have you ever considered asking them what more you can do for them?
3. Write out your own Love List and start living what you love to create more joy within. Try

writing out 100 things and start by doing 3 per day for a week and gradually increase from there.

CHAPTER 5

DAILY VIBES

Not so long ago, I was chatting with a lady who wanted to hire me for a medical intuitive assessment. She kept saying on the phone, "I don't know what's holding me back, probably myself!" I chuckled and said, "Yes, that is likely true."

Many people start the day vibrating low and continue throughout their day feeding that lower vibration. In a typical day, most people wake up to an alarm. An alarm tells you when to start the day, not your body. If the family is difficult to wake up and get ready, more frustration can be added to the rude alarm awakening. Before leaving the house, you may put up to 20 different chemicals on your body such as soap, shampoo, conditioner, deodorant, toothpaste, mouthwash, lotion, hair products, hairspray, perfume, eye shadow, eye liner, blush, foundation, lip stick, clothes that have chemicals on them from washing and drying, etc. All of these vibrate lower than your natural state.

Then, you might have a quick processed breakfast and coffee, because you are flying out the door, which also do not contribute to a higher vibration. You may ride a train, sit in traffic, or live in a city with lots of smog. Again, all of these things will decrease your vibration. Next, you may walk into a work situation that may be lacking in joy and mental stimulation, and that you really don't care for. You are just in this job for the pay cheque. You may surround yourself with people who are not vibrating high either. Lunch is quick and you may even nourish your body with a fresh salad. The vibe goes up and then possibly down as you wash it away with a mocha latte or a high sugar energy drink thinking that will keep you going.

Life after work may be filled with obligations of running your kids around. You love your kids, but secretly wish you were doing other things. You get home to cook a fast supper or maybe order a pizza. You get the family settled in for the night and watch some news on the TV, while having a large glass of wine. Then, you finally go to bed and do it all over again tomorrow.

If the above sounds familiar, then it's time to incorporate

higher vibes into your life. You are the only one who has control over this. Each one of us is capable of making greater decisions for our health and well-being.

When my client said that she thought she was holding herself back, she was right. We all do this. It may be in different ways, but we all make choices that block our own greatness. We can go on to blame others, but others are not responsible for our actions. We are only responsible for ourselves. (I am talking to myself here too!)

The great thing about it is that you have so much power within you; you only have to choose to do something different.

Here is an example of a higher vibrational day:

Wake up, do some stretches, have some quiet time (read, meditate etc.), and make a nutritious breakfast that the kids will wake up to. Have the kids' stuff prepped the night before, so that there is no rushed feeling to get them out the door. Walk or bike to work, if possible, to get some fresh air and movement in the body. If you drive, listen to an inspirational podcast, book (audible.com is awesome), or some uplifting music.

Work is an entire topic on its own. My wish for you is you find something you love that is meaningful in your life and that provides well for your family. If you do not have that, ask yourself what that would look like for you and start looking for it and visualizing it. We spend a lot of our lives at work; you are worthy enough to enjoy it!

Have your kids carpool with other friends to get them to their activities. Pick and choose which events you will attend and which events your children will be ok with on their own.

If you have a family, spend time in the evening bringing everyone together. Family units are becoming a rare thing. With the support of family, everyone does better in life and feels more connected, secure, and loved. This is a higher vibrational family unit. If a family just lives together without the connection of even a "Hey, how was your day?", there is an essential element of life missing, and it will trickle into adulthood. Connect, play, and converse with each other. This again raises the vibration. Making a meal is a great way to do that. Give everyone a job and start talking!

Put your feet up at the end of the day and relax. You've done well! Have a warm salt bath with your glass of wine and favourite music. Watch comedy if you like unwinding with TV. Laughter is a high vibration.

Connect with your partner. Sex is often left by the wayside as we become too busy or too tired to connect. How can you communicate more effectively? Do you need a date night?

Read before you go to bed. Consider staying off your

screens as much as possible as it has blue light that stimulates the nervous system and can keep you awake. Watch what you read and even what you place beside your bed as reading material, because everything holds a vibration. Even the clutter in your house is contributing to your vibration. Keep the clutter down and the tidiness up. Have a look at Marie Kondo's series on Netflix entitled, "Tidying Up with Marie Kondo" if you need some tips.

The last tip on vibrating higher would be to watch your thoughts. We are influenced heavily by our environment; therefore, it's important to surround ourselves with more positive energy. Meditation is one of the best ways to quiet your mind and introduce positive thoughts into your brain.

I know what you are thinking: "How the heck am I going to add one more thing into my life?" Here is my tip: when you shut your light off before you go to bed, place one hand on your heart and one on your abdomen and start saying in your mind all the things you are grateful for. Gratitude is the highest vibration on the planet, even higher than love. You may start by thanking the obvious, but then what about the not so obvious? What about things we take for granted in our lives like a pillow, food, a roof over our head, clothes to wear, fresh water, the ability to breathe, see, hear, etc. It's a great thing to practice before you go to sleep and even when you wake up and can't get back to sleep.

Thoughts to Ponder:

1. If a scale of 1-10 represented your vibration right now (10 being high), where would you be?
2. What can you change in your world (even if it's one thing) to increase your vibration?
3. What can you change in your family's world to increase your vibration?
4. Where in your life can you take more time to enjoy what is around you and delegate or stop the things that do not contribute to your higher vibration?

CHAPTER 6

READING PEOPLE

I have over 20 years of training with massage therapy, reiki, and medical intuition. As a result, I have been able to read the body muscularly, energetically, and emotionally. This may appear to be intimidating. I have heard of people scared to be around me or fearful to tell me things because they feel I will read them. While flattering, it isn't reality. If you and I are out for coffee, I am not going to tell you that I see your fourth chakra holding emotions of a painful loss and am experiencing chest pains that I believe are coming from you, and we need to clear that now! Even if I am experiencing these physical sensations, I am not going to read you unless you give me your consent and ask.

I am familiar with energy workers who will do this. I believe this is an unethical energy invasion of your privacy. At the same time, when a friend asks me if I can tune into their body, I usually do as I enjoy helping when I can.

It is not wise to just go around reading people's energy when they have not asked for this service. It would be like me massaging someone's body in public when they did not ask for it. "I just want to massage your left glute here as I'm sensing it's tight by the way you're walking." Would it help them? No! They did not ask for help. Healing can only begin by someone taking the responsibility of their own health and asking.

Everyone reads the vibration of energy. Most people just don't know what they are reading. For example, have you ever entered a room only to find the conversation stop and it suddenly feeling awkward? You may read that there was an argument going on and the air is tense! You feel that. Or, have you ever entered a party and there is laughter, fun, and joy felt everywhere? Yes, you can feel that, too. What about seeing a friend who looks tired and you start to yawn yourself? You feel all that as well. If you don't believe me, go to a funeral and tell me what you feel. Yes, that is energy too. If you are feeling it, you are reading it. There is no difference between you and me. I may have strengthened my intuitive muscle with my training and by practicing with it everyday, but you can easily read energy too.

I believe reading energy can be our superpower! Energy is felt through vibrations that your body is reading and interpreting. Since the body is the interpreter, I can't stress enough how important it is to get to know your own body. I will write about that at greater length in a later chapter, but for now, become friends with your body! Spend time with it, and ask it questions. This is why meditation has become so valuable. People are spending time learning who they are so that they can know how to interpret all that is coming at them, including the energetic vibrations.

How can you tell if you are picking up someone else's energy? You first need to know what is normal for you and when you feel your best. Knowing your normal state is as easy as getting out in nature and acknowledging how you feel. Breathe in fresh air and surround yourself with a lake, mountains, or trees. You can also spend time alone getting to know who you are. This will help you to connect to Source energy (God, Universe, Creator, #callitwhatyouwant) long enough for you to feel what's happening in your own body.

One of the craziest experiences of energy exploration I had was travelling on public transit in London, England. My husband and I would take the train downtown and do some exploring, see a show, or just go and wander around. This was exciting since there was always something new to see. Multiple times, while riding the train, my stomach would start to churn and I would feel really sick. It ruined my time. I would plough through the pain, but I was not myself and I didn't know why.

When I began to think about it, I realized this also happened several times when I was a child. I hated being in large crowds or in a hot and stuffy house at family gatherings. In my twenties, I also remember feeling ill around certain people. Sometimes, I would even excuse myself because I felt ill, even though I had no reason to feel sick. In these times, I had no idea what my normal was or what was happening internally. Today, I know that my body was giving me messages from reading the energy of others around me.

With regards to my body on the train ride, there were likely other people's energies that were vibrating in my energy field. If you think about it, how many people ride the train daily, weekly, monthly, and yearly? How many have even sat in the seat I chose? Surrounded by millions of people with energies interconnecting, how can we only operate on our own when we are continually crossing energy fields with people on a daily basis?

I have a few young clients who are sensitive to energy and a family member who I believe has these sensitivities too. It's not a bad thing; we just need to know what to do with the message that our body is reading.

The first thing is to keep our bodies as strong as we can with the basics that we talked about in the last chapter. Keeping our vibration high and operating out of love is really our best defence. When we are tired, malnourished, dehydrated, angry, or fearful, it is quite simple to attract a lower vibration, because that is how we are vibrating too.

One of the easiest tricks I have learned about feeling another person's energy comes from Access Consciousness™. They teach that when you feel off and not yourself, you begin by stating, "Who does this belong to? Return to sender with consciousness attached." I have also imagined this energy from others being put into a huge cylinder with sharp teeth that mulch and transform that energy into love. I see hearts coming out of the bottom of it when it has been transformed. Why not transform this energy into love so that it can do good instead of returning it to the person who may just keep recirculating it on the planet? Sounds too simple? You must try it. I use this statement every day when I work on people as my body is continually feeling other people's energy.

There are times when you may need other tools such as smudge. Smudging is used by many cultures in rituals and ceremonies to clear energy of negativity, fear, anxiety, grief, and depression. There may also be times when you need an energy worker to assist you. It is not weak to ask for help.

One of my other go-to statements that helps with clearing the energy of others is, "Any energy that is in or around my energy field that does not belong to me, you need to leave now. Any psychic daggers that I have thrown or have been thrown at me, you need to dissolve now." I say this every night. You can create your own power statements to help with unwanted energy.

Knowing your body and how it feels in a normal state will allow you to recognize if you are being influenced by another person's state. Then, by using one of the tools previously mentioned, you can become aware of it, send that energy back to the person, or transmute it for good.

Thoughts to Ponder:

1. Have you felt signals that your body has tried giving you when hanging out with certain people or possibly even in certain buildings?

2. Do you know your own normal state of being? I challenge you to spend time with yourself, possibly out in nature, and find your normal state. Use your senses to feel and strive to commune with yourself every chance you get!

3. You may feel the energy others are giving off, but what about you? What are you sending out there into the world of vibrations?

CHAPTER 7

THE ENERGY OF FRIENDSHIPS

When I was in my 20's, I thought I would have all my friends for life. At that time, having lots of close friends and socializing seemed very important. Twenty years later, I do value my social life and my friends, but they definitely have changed. Now, I have more acquaintances than friends. Even though my close circle of friends is much smaller, we are a lot more intimate with what we share.

My first encounter with several friends falling away from my life came when my first husband and I were divorcing. It's strange how many people feel like they need to decide whom they will support when a relationship ends. My friends were no different. I felt extremely left out of our friend circle when this happened. It was very painful to experience this isolation.

At the same time, new friendships were developing. People who I didn't even think would become my friends came into my life and supported me. Many were there just for a season and some are still around today. I appreciate each one greatly.

Looking back on this time, I am actually thankful for some of the people who are no longer in my life. Back then, I was an entirely different person. Having my world shaken up made me find out who I really was, and it helped make me who I am today. I know for a fact that the people who were in my life then would not be able to relate or support me today, because our beliefs are entirely different.

The saying is true: people come and go through our lives for a reason, a season, or a lifetime. Some people I thought would be there for a lifetime all of a sudden left and I had no idea why. I have had ex-friends express an almost repulsion towards me, and I have no idea what caused it. I do know that our vibrations no longer match, and there was no other choice but to go our separate ways.

This cannot be labelled as right or wrong; it just is. The whole saying, "Who cares what people think of me?" applies. Still, we all care. If we take a deeper look at the big picture and remember how like energy attracts like energy, we can deal with the loss of friendship a little easier. Remembering that we are always being looked after by Source helps too.

On the flip side, I have also left friendships. Leaving any type of relationship is usually triggered by a crossed boundary, unmet expectations, or anger. All the while, it is the vibration that is no longer connecting. We are no longer on the same radio frequency. For example, I had a newer friendship with a lovely woman who was helping me train to walk a marathon. Every day we would walk along the river accompanied by her beautiful Black Labrador. We socialized together and our husbands met. We really enjoyed each other's company.

She had some mental issues and told me she had attempted to commit suicide a few times. We talked about suicide and I felt we were quite open with the heavy subject. Months went on and she began cancelling our friendship dates. I didn't understand why, and I was starting to get a little annoyed. I snapped on her one day for not showing up for her scheduled massage. She promised not to do it again. The last straw was when she stood me up on my birthday lunch. It was quite embarrassing sitting in a restaurant waiting for her. When she did not show, I was furious! It was MY birthday. (That was the year that I decided to spend my birthdays doing the things I love without the expectation of others.)

It turned out that she had attempted suicide the night before. I didn't even know how to respond to that. I was still mad, but, at the same time, I felt sad for my friend.

Weeks passed and we made plans to meet. It was a coffee date like no other. It was as though the Divine was looking out for both of our highest interests. We talked about my birthday, and she apologized. I listened to her speak about why, and felt her struggle. Then, I spoke and felt like something greater was taking over my body. I felt like I was suspended from the ceiling and was watching myself break up with my friend. There was such strength in my words. I didn't even cry though my heart ached for her. I told her I didn't know how to be a friend to her and thought it was best if we ended our friendship.

I drove away from that encounter both relieved and ashamed. It was the weirdest feeling. I believed our vibrations could no longer sustain our relationship. It appears a bit selfish when you read this, and yet I trust that we were both being looked after for our highest good. I also didn't want to judge her for her struggles or for her missed dates. It was a very hard and confusing time, but it wasn't an isolated incident in my life. The same scenario happened again a few years later.

I worked for a college and found out through another teacher that we were not getting paid for the semester. The school was low on funds. I felt that the director was a bit dishonest in her actions. She promised to pay (she still hasn't as I'm typing this a year later). I felt used and devalued, as there was no fair exchange in our services. I told her I was unwilling to work until payment was received. The conversation at the restaurant got quite loud with my announcement to quit. I experienced the same 'out-of-body-floating' feeling again. In fact, I recall my humanness was telling my spirit to "Shut up. Shut up. Shut up!" My spirit took over and very calmly, without drama or tears, explained the unfairness, and that I was done.

These two similar yet very different situations made me realize there was something greater than me looking out for my well-being. In both situations, I felt as if I was suspended from the ceiling and something other than my humanness took over. The vibrations of these relationships were so uncomfortable that the only thing left to do was end them. I feel that my spirit ended them, because my physical body and mind would have stayed in the relationships longer. This was not for my highest good. I can see that now.

Do I hate these women? Not at all. I believe everyone in my life is a teacher. These women came into my life for a reason. I am thankful for both of these situations and all that they have taught me. I likely would not be where I am today without them.

This past year I had three experiences where forgiveness was asked for and an understanding was met. Lack of

48

forgiveness is a destructive vibration that can hold you back and even cause physical symptoms. There are many views on what forgiveness is, and if it is valuable to one another. I believe forgiveness is only for you. It is to disconnect the energy cord that is causing mental havoc and restore the natural flow of energy to your being. When there is someone in my life who is constantly on my mind (usually in a not so nice way), I know it would serve me to forgive.

When I work on this, I start to explore my own shadow. You can research the work of Dr. John Demartini, Debbie Ford, and Deepak Chopra to learn more on this subject. Most of us don't even want to go there, because we have these beliefs that we are perfect and the other person is evil. When you can get to the trigger of what another person has set off in you, you can begin to explore how you do the same in others. You may be thinking, "How is it possible that another may cheat, steal, or lie?" We all do in different ways. When we uncover this, we understand the person we are struggling with in a much deeper way and it dissolves the trigger. This helps release the energy cord that holds us back from our potential.

It is fascinating work that needs more explanation than what I am allowing here. It will open up your world to see how each unpleasant encounter we have can be the greatest teacher. There is always a greater picture to your life than just the physical.

Thoughts to Ponder:

1. Are there relationships in your life where people left because you had different vibrations? Who are they? Take a deep look into the why and thank them for what they have taught you.

2. What are these relationships teaching you about yourself?

3. Look up these authors and their work with the shadow: Deepak Chopra, Debbie Ford, Byron Katie, and Dr. John Demartini. You may choose to buy a journal and start exploring your experiences in a deeper way.

CHAPTER 8

THE ENERGY OF FAMILY

You begin learning from your family as soon as you are born. You adopt beliefs, behaviours, and coping skills. Then, you pass those along to your children. Along the way, you have either adopted what your parents have taught you or you have learned your own way in raising children and living as a unit.

Some of my teachings have suggested that we choose our family before we are born to learn the lessons that we came here to experience. This is an interesting thought that can be neither proved nor disproved, but fascinating to think of when your family drives you nuts!

It feels as though children are possibly holding up a

mirror to what is really going on in our own lives. This mirror is awakening our awareness in such a way that we can no longer hide from our wounds and rejections in life. We are constantly being shown how to be more authentic.

Some time ago, I worked on a seven-year-old who had anxiety. How in the heck does a seven-year-old get anxiety? The medical system can make you believe that this child is lacking anti-anxiety medication. I don't personally believe this is the solution. We must start by looking at the energy of the environment that this little one comes from. From my observation, it felt as though she was mimicking what was going on in her family. When you think of it, being born with anxiety seems more unlikely than copying someone's actions in the family unit.

Parents have brought their children to see me because of mental conditions that they believe are the result of stress or the child not knowing how to deal with stress. In my opinion, it's not the kids that are stressed. It's the busyness of the family unit that is stressing the entire family out! YOU ARE TOO BUSY! A child, from my experience, often mimics the energetic and physical surroundings in the home environment. It is from these surroundings or the family's lifestyle that helps or hinders a child to go to school and function. When they are older, it's the tools they have learned at home that will be useful to navigate the world as a functional adult.

What are we teaching them?

What is the energy of busy? It's chaos, stress, and lack of connection as you run from here to there. It's financial stress created from being away every weekend with activities and sports. It's physical stress resulting from not eating, sleeping, or drinking what your body needs to keep up with this pace. And, it's spiritual stress created from the minimal connection with your soul or with each other. Whatever happened to family night, kids just playing in the yard, or hanging out with friends? What I often see are families running around like chickens with their heads cut off.

It's time to calm the f@$% down! Just take a look at your life. Yes, you may see that everyone around you is living in this pace and surviving. There is a difference between surviving and thriving! You always have a choice.

I think the most damaging thing that we are showing our children is this is the pace at which they should live. Kids only do as they are taught until they see another way to do it. Are you duplicating what your parents believed and have possibly shown you? Did someone call you lazy when you sat still for a minute to catch your breath, and then you vowed you would never be lazy?

Recently, one of my clients told me that she is trying to teach her daughter self-care techniques while her daughter is still at home. I applauded her!!! (I think I clapped out loud.) This is very rare and very needed. This parent understands the importance of thriving because of personal experience, and is making it a priority to do yoga with her daughter at night. They also schedule family time, and she is teaching the child how to rest. Also, remember self-care is impossible to teach if one does not practice these values themselves.

Can you imagine when your child is in university or the work force and life presents hardship? It will happen. It's only a matter of time. What skills will they have learned from you to cope and adapt? Will they have learned that when life is tough they have permission to eat, drink, or do drugs to numb the pain? What can you teach them while they are in your care?

Another scenario that I see a lot in my office is people of all ages who are almost afraid of the silence. The silence is where the larger issues in life come up and are just waiting to be addressed by you. People become very uncomfortable with the thoughts in their mind. When we skirt around them or shove them under the rug, they just keep coming up. They want to be looked at and dealt with. When we continually ignore them, they may even show up as pain or disease in the body. We will discuss this further in later chapters.

If silence triggers you, start a conversation with your body and soul and ask it what it wants to tell you. Until you become completely happy being alone in quiet, you will have things to address in your life. Why address them?

Because doing so leads to peace. You are worthy of a peaceful life! Your kids are deserving of knowing how to attain peace in their lives by you teaching them what has worked for you. It's you who needs to do the work to show them how; otherwise, they may never know what just being feels like and how they attain contentment.

Not sure where to start? You may need a professional to help you with the heavier issues, but try five minutes with just you alone with no noise. You are not allowed to do anything but just be. Form a habit by doing this for 21 days. If five minutes of stillness is hard for you, tap into your senses and take note of what you feel, hear, see, and smell. By tuning into your senses, you come to the present moment. There is nowhere else you need to be or can be.

You may think about joining a meditation class. You could even make it a family outing. Connecting to yourself does not have to be that structured. You could enjoy a walk, a Sunday drive, a luxurious bath, or sitting on your deck listening to music while drinking a beer. Tune in to your body and observe what is cluttering your mind.

I've heard it said that anxiety comes from living in the future and depression comes from living in the past. Can you imagine how many mental health issues we would solve if we knew how to live in the present and taught our children to do the same?

Calm down your home environment. You are worth it! Do it for your children's health and your sanity. This rant from a non-parent is over!

Thoughts to Ponder:

1.   When was the last time your family just hung out, laughed, and played together in your home? You can apply this to your partner too.

2.   What can you teach your child to help with stress now so that in the future they will have some tools to navigate through life?

3.   Are you comfortable in silence? Have you asked yourself why you may not be? Are you willing to carve out five minutes a day to become friends with silence and the present moment?

4.   Is there anything that you need to address in your inner world? (e.g. relationship conflicts, feelings of rejection, abandonment from family, abuse, etc.) Professional help is not a weakness and is available to help you when you are ready to help yourself.

CHAPTER 9

THE ENERGY OF TRUST

When we wake up from our slumber, we have a pretty good idea of what our day will look like. Each hour is planned out including the kids' schedules, meals, and activities. All of this makes up your day. What happens when the day throws you a curve ball? Maybe you get fired or your son gets suspended from school or your spouse gets hurt at work or your aging parents need your help. This is where life gets a little interesting and the perfect plan you had for your day goes up in smoke!

What we deem as wrong or not in our plans can often be one of the greatest blessings. I have heard of people getting hurt at work and going to the hospital only to find out that they have cancer and need to start treatment as soon as possible. Is the accident then considered bad, or possibly life-saving? I have heard of people who have died only to be able to donate their organs to multiple people to save lives. Is the death labelled bad or good? I have heard of people who have gone bankrupt in their business only to find their dream job that provides more enjoyment. Is the bankruptcy good or bad?

If you take the labels off of the life event and step back from the moment, you may even begin to understand this universe a bit better. You may begin to feel like you have been looked after all along. Take, for instance, the last time your life was in crisis. What happened? Are you okay now? Do you still consider it as a crisis?

When you see these huge life events as a change in the path - a change in energy - you do not have to give them the labels of good or bad. They just are. When disaster strikes, if you can remember the last time crisis hit and how looked after you were, you will gain the strength to remember that this, too, will pass and all will be well once again.

Trusting that invisible energy (calling it whatever you want) will move you towards a greater understanding of your mission in life. Years ago, I remember trying to get a small business loan to do a $30,000 renovation at my office. The bank required quotes from the contractors. In fact, they wanted 3 quotes for each job by different contractors. I live in a small town and to even find the contractors proved difficult, not to mention three plumbers, electricians, and drywallers! I had one or two job quotes and was feeling entirely frustrated. I decided to just surrender- not as in give up what I wanted - but surrender to the fact that I wasn't in control of this project.

I remember thinking this while driving one day. I literally threw my hands in the air and said, "If this job is to be done, you are going to have to help me sort out the details." I drove around the block and marched into the bank.

By coincidence or fate, my banker wasn't busy and saw me right away. I told her what I had, the difficulty in finding quotes, and that I estimated I needed $30,000 based on our last renovation. I then asked what more I needed to do to make this happen. I walked out of the bank with the money promised to my account within a week. How did that happen? Luck? Fortune? Or was it the power of surrender and asking for help from an unseen source?

There is an invisible force out there that wants to help us through life. We try to do things on our own and most times it's not in the perfect timing of the Divine. I think about this when I lose my keys or stub my toe in a rush. Is there a perfect timing in the orchestra of my own life that is making me slow down for a few seconds because what lies ahead is not ready for me?

We have all heard about people who were not at the tragic event and would have died if they hadn't slept in or missed the train or decided to take a different route to work that day. Were they being watched over?

This is all part of a larger picture of energy. We can manipulate some of the details in our physical life, but when we become aware of something greater than the physical, we start to realize that there is a much larger screenplay going on around us.

Thoughts to Ponder:

1. What do you deem a crisis in your life now or in the past? Have you seen a glimpse of being looked after, cared for, or loved by physical and non-physical energy?
2. What do you call this higher power? Have you acknowledged it? What is it for you?
3. Have you surrendered to the possibilities of something greater having your back?
4. What would it take for you to ask for help in life?

PART 2

THE ENERGY OF BUSINESS

Your time is limited, so don't waste it living someone else's life. Don't be trapped by dogma – which is living with the results of other people's thinking. Don't let the noise of others' opinions drown out your own inner voice. And most important, have the courage to follow your heart and intuition.

~ Steve Jobs

CHAPTER 10

THE ENERGY OF COWORKERS

We all need people in our life and yet, escaping to a small cabin in the country with no outside contact is sometimes so appealing that I have actually researched the possibilities on Google! People provide the greatest human experiences and, unfortunately, they also provide the greatest misery. Thankfully, we have the power to effectively pick and choose our company and, for the most part, we all decide whom to spend time with. Many of us don't believe we have these choices. We do.

For instance, if your family is always complaining and asking you for help or money, it creates an energy drain. This often happens when the other person is not a match to your energy vibration and taking more than they are giving. The good news is that you can choose how much time you spend in their company.

It is harder in work situations where you see a person everyday and they do not jive at all with your energy. In fact, they may severely piss you off. Then what? Awareness is the first thing to pay attention to. Just observe it. Ask yourself if you are possibly seeing your reflection in them; there may be something in your life that needs your attention. In the energy world, this is called projecting. If you are projecting something onto them, it is a sign your soul is asking for some self-healing. They could be also be projecting something onto you, and need their own self-reflection. Most people are too unaware to take a serious look at what this may mean personally.

Dr. John Demartini has a brilliant method for diffusing the triggers you may find in others. He gets a person to write out what action they are struggling with, and then asks them to take a look at their own life and see where they may have responded similarly. When they see that the other person is doing the best that they know how, they understand that we are ultimately all one and the same.

Here is an example: You find one of your co-workers super annoying. They are always cutting you off when you speak. They never seem to listen or ask questions, and just talk about themselves and how great they are.

When you recognize the trigger of annoying, ask yourself if they are a reflection of your own behaviour. It is really hard to see sometimes since we always think we are right and want to appear as such. Take a good look in the mirror they are holding up and see if there is something you can learn. If there isn't, ask yourself what else in their behaviour is triggering you. Is there someone in your life that you are not giving your full attention to, or do you not feel heard in your marriage or family? When people irritate you, there is almost always something to learn from them. The deeper the irritation is, the greater the learning.

Another example is when you are the manager of a younger staff that is mostly concerned with having fun with a project, time off, or social interaction. You are all about productivity and getting things done. What they may be showing you is that you could use some play time and lightening up. You may also be in their life to show structure and how to succeed in the work force. You are both contributing to each other's lives. One only needs to start becoming aware of the messages around them by paying attention to the energy exchange with others.

An important point is to allow others to be themselves without personal judgment. Judgment really is the poison of our society. We have all judged and have all felt judged. This energy is heavy and useless. It does nothing but inflate our egos for a brief moment. Try to be the observer without the judgment and just see how that works for you. You may start to break the unconscious cycle of judgment when you become the observer.

It's interesting to hang out with people who judge a lot. I have a friend who will make four or five statements of what is wrong with people or things in a single breath. I have learned not to respond by saying, "Yeah, you are right" or "Yes, that is wrong," since right and wrong are judgments too. This diffuses the judgments for a while.

This person feeds her ego on feeling better about herself and feeling right about herself when she judges everyone and everything else. It is unconscious and not on purpose; it just is. When I realized that, I realized I do not have to judge her for her comments. I accept her for who she is. When I choose acceptance over judgment, I am no longer triggered by her comments.

Let's flip this conversation to recognize the energy of people you are really attracted to. This doesn't have to be romantic attraction, but it can be. Think about how you became friends with a stranger or co-worker. How did you two find each other? There was a vibration almost like a beacon call that was put out and answered.

Recently, I taught a Reiki class and had two beautiful women join me. The women worked together and didn't really know each other, but sensed from each other warmth, love, and acceptance. When we shine our light bright and vibrate high, other higher vibrating souls are attracted to us. When we vibrate in a confused state of wanting to be authentic, yet dumb ourselves down in order to fit in with the people around us, we attract confused souls. Similarly, we may attract people with negative vibes when our attitude projects that everything and everyone is foolish, wrong, or stupid. We can see that vibrating in a non-judgmental state is more attractive and appealing.

Another interesting vibrational exchange in business is having a poor vibration when advertising. This will not help to achieve what you desire with your marketing.

A few years ago, we had a wonderful co-worker decide to leave our office for a new job. We were sad, heartbroken, and a bit angry. We spent a lot of time and effort training her, and our clients really loved her. Somehow, in a ridiculous way, we always think we will retire before our staff does. We placed an ad in a couple of places for a replacement while we were feeling a lot of those negative vibrations, and guess what we received in resumes? There were people who had little to no experience, people who didn't own their own phone and had no way to be reached, and people who didn't show up for an interview. It really was a disaster.

I said to my husband, "We need to change our vibrations, because the right person is out there. We are just tuned into the wrong frequency! We can attract our next amazing staff member; we just need to change our channel."

We changed it up and focused our energy on all that we wanted in the next receptionist. We thought about her qualities and how she would present to clients and us. Facebook was our friend and sure enough we attracted a fantastic co-worker who worked out perfectly. What a change when WE decided to vibrate higher! You can do this too.

Your business holds pieces of your own vibration. When people say that you have put your blood, sweat, and tears into a project or business, they really mean energy. For this reason, we must keep our own vibrations in check within a business and the vibrations of those who we have work with us. Numerous times we have hired because the position is empty and we never considered the energy of the person filling it. In the future, we will ask if the applicant's energy will add or take away from the business.

There are many companies who do profile checks on a new employee's personality, but they never stop to consider the energy of the person, or how they will fit in with the rest of the team. I am reminded of one woman, in particular, who I hired to do massage. She had her own business and was already quite established. She was a great therapist, but not really a team player. She eventually left and I was a bit surprised at how happy my co-workers were upon her departure. I didn't realize how they struggled with her, because she wasn't willing to take part in a team atmosphere and preferred to do her own thing. I wasn't aware of the importance in the energy of hiring her and how she would (or wouldn't) fit in with others.

Another woman I worked with was hired for her reception abilities only to find that she was horrible at her job. The office was so stuck for a receptionist that she was kept on longer than she should have been. In her parting she was a crying mess because she thought this was her dream job.

The business felt funny after she left and when my intuitive friend tuned in, she saw that this particular receptionist cursed the staff and the business. It may not have even been intentional or conscious, but her energy was angry that we let her go and she projected that anger onto us and the business. When we released that negative vibration with commanding statements, the office felt much clearer and happier.

Some of the commanding statements we used that you can adapt for your own purposes were: "Any residual energy that is left behind by (insert name) that is not based in love, you need to leave. Any curse or bad feelings that (insert name) projected on this business, building, co-workers, or boss that does not serve our highest potential, you need to leave now." Smudge may also help. You can also open windows and light candles to increase the energy in the office. You can even add a vase of fresh cut flowers.

I know this seems crazy since you cannot see energy, but you sure can feel it. We are all energy, and we are powerful without even realizing it. Just think about where you work and how many people have gone through the doors, including clients, customers, and staff. There are hundreds, possibly thousands, and maybe more! How many have loved it and how many have cursed the staff, boss, business, or the building?

If you have someone else in your office that understands energy as you do and is willing to be present while stating these sentences, it will have a stronger effect. Stand in your power. You deserve to have a comfortable energetic work environment.

Thoughts to Ponder:

1. Who in your life do you need to spend less time with or practice extreme self-care around? Who takes more than they give in your world?

2. Who is being a mirror in your life? Who irritates the crap out of you? What are they teaching you by their behaviours? Where are you being the same?

3. What are the vibes you are sending into the world? Are you happy with what you are attracting or do you need to change the channel?

4.   Does your building need to be cleared of past energies? Are you confident to do this yourself? If not, you can hire an energy worker to assist you.

CHAPTER 11

THE ENERGY OF SPACE

In the last chapter we briefly covered the importance of energy when hiring. There is a lot more you can do energetically to influence your business. I will share with you my experience from working with others and owning my own massage therapy business and wellness centre.

In the early days of my career, I had no say in the energy of the business since I worked for someone else. I did have a say in my own energy and how I presented it to the business, but the building, hiring of staff, and even the treatment rooms were all the owner's personal energy.

My first massage practice was in a chiropractic office and I basically came in and did my work, then left. At first, the clients I saw were attracted to the business' energy (the physical space), and the doctors' energies. We shared many clients. The clients who I started developing relationships with (the ones that were rebooking with me) were attracted to my energy and skills. For the first couple of years, this worked for both of us.

Eventually, our work environment became uncomfortable. My energy was attracting clientele interested in stress management, while the doctors in the office were focused on attracting clientele interested in pain management. It wasn't long before I was being asked to market to people who were not my ideal clients, and this made an even more tense work environment.

Today, this all makes sense when I look at it from an energetic standpoint. At the time, it was like I was going through a crisis. I couldn't understand why I was so unhappy. I was already starting my journey into stress management and I was drawn to and loved working with the stressed-out clients who were eager to de-stress. I was not really enjoying the people came to me with specific physical conditions who only wanted me to manage their pain. This caused a clash of energies internally within the office. Eventually, I chose to leave.

Today, I have 100% say in my business and I even own the building I practice in. Every aspect is in my control to change. This can be an intimidating thought because if a person doesn't like something or feels funky in the space, it is heavily my responsibility to check in and see what's going on both energetically and physically.

Through all the years that led up to my current business, I have learned some very valuable lessons. First, ask yourself who you want to cater to in your practice/business. Who is your ideal client? Traditional business training calls this your target market. Once you know who this is, it makes all marketing and decisions quite a bit easier. You do not have to market yourself to the world, because not everyone is your ideal client or customer.

Secondly, does the company share your passion? Are you the right fit? Can you honestly wake up each day and be excited to go to work? Do you share the same vision that your company does?

Today, my ideal client is someone who is completely stressed out by life, who has maybe had a breakdown, lost a loved one, or is working through tough conditions such as cancer. I love these clients, as well as the ones who want to maintain their health with massage or energy work! This is my calling and I have the tools to help. I provide a calming space to listen, a moment to breathe, and the skills to relax the body so that the mind has a better chance of processing all that is going on.

Once you realize who your ideal client is, then look at ways that you can best attract them into your business. All businesses only have a few seconds to make a great impression. This starts with how easy it is to find you and the simplicity required to book an appointment or purchase your goods. Is it a frustrating experience or a smooth one? I'm not the only one who has been on a website and has had to quit the purchase process, because it was too stupid or too long of an ordeal. How frustrating!

Also, ensure there is an easy way to reach you. Have you ever tried to leave a message and it takes weeks before your message is returned or there isn't even an answering service to pick up your message? What kind of energy are you attracting when you are operating a business that is difficult to engage with?

Once your customer arrives into your business, what are their senses going to experience? Is the space aesthetically pleasing or is it cluttered, dirty, or dated? Who is greeting the customers or clients, and is it friendly or rushed? Does the staff make eye contact and treat the client with respect? Is the consumer directed to what will happen next and where to go?

I have received over a thousand massages in my lifetime and I can't tell you how many rooms I have been in that are unclean or so small and congested that the therapist actually moves the table while I'm on it. Worse yet, I feel their boobs touch my body because they are unaware of their surroundings or have no space to work in. (Yes, these are real experiences!)

I have come across very unfriendly people in the service industry. I have been short changed on time for a service. I have experienced stained and smelly linens while receiving a massage and even had a therapist blowing their nose while I was receiving a massage and not bothering to go wash their hands. The environment that you offer up to people holds a vibration and this is what will attract or repel your ideal client or customer.

Have you ever experienced anxiety from clutter? I have experienced this from a retail store in my area. A few people have told me that they cannot go into the store, because, they too, feel overwhelming anxiety. It's crowded and two people cannot be in the same aisle together. One day I was in there with my mom. I became so overwhelmed that I told her I was returning to the car. I just couldn't do it and, truthfully, the shopping experience wasn't very fun for me. How your place of work makes someone feel will have the power to make or break a sale.

Possibly you can relate this to your own business or your own experiences. Does your space need some energetic attention? Are there places you may choose to stay away from because your body is uncomfortable or it is not fun for you?

If you do not have control over your business or office in the way an entrepreneur does, you can still do a few things to increase the energy of your space.

Start with your desk area. When an area is organized and tidy, the energy of the space flows in a different way than when it is cluttered or dirty. This is an easy and cheap experiment to try. Display pictures that bring you joy (travel pics, family pics, pet pics). If there are objects that bring you joy, place them in the office or on your desk. Keep your office clean, organized, and tidy. Open a window if possible. Crystals, salt lamps, candles, music, or plants will also help raise the energy of your space.

Love your furniture in your space and replace any broken or worn out pieces. Make sure the flow is set up to allow for ease of movement. For example, does a person have to move around your desk to sit down?

Have a pleasant answering message on your phone and record it when you are in a good mood and smiling. If you can, paint the wall color a refreshing color that allows you to work with ease and not be distracted. Each of these things will allow more energy to flow in your space.

If you get stuck, ask someone how it feels in your space. Ask for advice on decorating from a Feng Shui specialist. You may also want to hire a secret shopper to call your business and set up an appointment just to test the energy of ease. This is a valuable way to learn what a client or customer will experience.

You may find that you have more control over your space than you think. By letting the energy flow and enjoying your space, you will attract the clientele and customers that you want! You will be setting your environment up to allow the flow of abundance in all ways.

Thoughts to Ponder:

1. Do you like your work? Is it time to move on or make some changes?
2. Do you like your workspace?
3. What do you have control of to change? Where can you make some changes, even today?
4. Is your space clean and tidy? Do you need to hire help to decorate or clean?

CHAPTER 12

THE BUSINESS' ENERGY

N ow that you know some tips to help the energy flow in your physical space, let's talk about the energy created by the people in your business. We'll start with you, since you are the most important energy attractor or repellent in your life.

Many business books will tell you all the ways to advertise your services and products from business cards to Facebook advertising to brochures and sandwich boards. Is this all there is to it? A specific advertising budget and plan? There are many ways to show the world who you are.

For years in my community, there was a self-taught

healer who lived on a remote farm. He did no advertising, barely took appointments, had no online presence, and didn't have what some would even call a business; yet, he was so busy that people just found him.

How was this possible? I believe word of mouth was very powerful for him. It was also his personal energy that was drawing people to his business. He was a very kind, gentle soul who had a deep desire and calling to help people. I love his example of just being who you are meant to be, with no hidden agendas, and a mad passion to help people. It's not always this simple, but this example does provide a few things we can learn from.

In my own practice, I have made it important to develop nurturing business relationships. These are not friendships or romantic. These are client-therapist relationships that are in a category all of their own. There is a huge element of trust, care, and concern for their well-being. I make it a priority to have strong client-therapist relationships and, because of it, my schedule is full most days. I love my clients and they make my day very enjoyable!

On the days when my schedule isn't full, I trust the Divine is taking care of the larger picture. Sometimes I need a break and my schedule truly does open. Once I over-booked myself when I decided to teach a weekly energy class after my scheduled day of massage. It wasn't until I made the commitment that I realized how full one particular day was. I wasn't sure how to handle it. I didn't want to cancel on anyone, and I had nowhere to move them. I was prepared to take one hour at a time and power through. To my delight, someone was sick. It sounds horrible to say, but it helped my day tremendously.

Sometimes, I am being looked after in a different way that has little to do with me. I have witnessed many times a short notice cancellation that may be tricky to fill and then moments later (as short as 2 minutes) a person in dire need is asking to get in. They are shocked to be able to come in a couple of hours. This whole business and energy thing is interesting to watch if we do not force or manipulate it.

In the beginning of my career, when my day was slim with little to no bookings or if I came to work with a few cancellations, a panic and fear would take over my body and mind. I would start to play crazy stories in my mind wondering if I could pay my bills, if I was in the wrong career, or if I would be able to survive. It is a horrible feeling coming from this place of lack and unworthiness. I believe many people get stuck in this thinking only to create more of it (your energy attracts more of whatever you focus on).

To get out of this circle of fear, one has to fake it until you make it. It really does start with mindset and belief. When you are struggling, it is hard to find that belief within you. One of my go-to mind strategies is "If they can do it, I can do it; there is no difference between them and me."

I have also surrounded myself with people who believe in me and my abilities which helps tremendously. That supportive encouragement can strengthen your mindset to help you reach another level of success. Meditation is also a key factor in strengthening your mind and showing you more of how to trust the perfect flow of energy in your business and all of life.

An example of trusting the flow was shown to me recently through a long-term client named Melissa. She is also a business owner and understands this energy concept with schedules, flow, and trusting what will be will be.

Melissa messaged me on a Thursday and asked if she could come earlier the following Monday. I replied that at the moment my schedule was full and I was unable to move her appointment, but if something came up, I'd let her know. She responded by saying, "I thought that would be the case, but I am just putting it out there."

Here is the crazy part. My schedule was packed that day, and low and behold, the client scheduled before her cancelled. When I texted Melissa the news of the cancellation, I also jokingly told her to quit manipulating my schedule like that! We laughed about it, but it really can be that simple. If you need an appointment or a change of one (or anything in life for that matter) just put it out there. We forget we have this energetic superpower! Everything is energy. Remember that always. Melissa has manipulated my schedule about four times now. She gets it!

Other times, I am looking at my week's schedule and there is one spot that hasn't filled yet. The entire week and the next are filled, but this one-hour appointment is just wide open. I often use Facebook to relay my schedule to clients, and so I may post the spot is available or I may just leave it. The majority of times a person will find it. I have asked in my mind, "I wonder who is looking for a massage?" or "I wonder who needs a massage today?" The person who comes is in so much need for TLC that it's like the appointment was made just for them. How does that happen? I believe it is all energy and the vibration of the intention to fill these appointments with a person who needs it.

Your business may be trying to communicate something to you. It possibly might be saying that you need a break or that you need to change something. The business may want to create something else to serve people in another way. I have some friends who literally talk to their businesses like another human. "Sweet business, what would you like to create today?" "How much should we raise our rates this year?" Or, "Would you like to host this class?" Your business holds an energy vibration just like you do. Remember, all things in the universe vibrate.

How well is your business vibrating? Do you fight it when it is showing you something for your greater good?

There have been many times when I didn't listen to my business. I remember having a look at our financial statements and seeing that our original business plan was no longer working. I ignored it and kept struggling. Later, through a coaching program, it was mentioned to me that we needed to change up the structure of the therapists in order to be profitable - not more profitable, but to actually be profitable. I fought that assessment hard and said that if we changed, there would be no therapists left... and to quit messing with my dream 'yada-yada-yada' (insert all my excuses).

Sometime later, I had a colleague interested in buying the business and when she looked at the numbers, she said they didn't make sense and that the business was not making money. It was then that I realized it was time for me to take a better look at what was going on. My business was trying hard to get my attention and I was not listening to what needed to be done.

Finally, I listened and started a conversation with my business as to what it really wanted. Today, it is not the same business, but much more profitable and enjoyable. Gosh, why do we take so long to change, especially when it is for our own good? Our businesses are looking out for us. We just have to make sure we take time to listen to what they are saying energetically.

Thoughts to Ponder:

1. How does your business feel to others? Ask a friend or your closest clients if you have no idea. Do people want to come and do business with you because they love being in your space, or does it repel clients to get in and get out or maybe not come in at all?

2. Do you converse with your business? What has it been saying? I challenge you to spend a few minutes every day asking it what it wants and then be brave enough to make some changes.

CHAPTER 13

THE ENERGY OF SOCIAL MEDIA

Internet advertising of any form was not around when I started my career as a massage therapist. In the early days, I remember creating and photocopying flyers and handing them out in my neighbourhood to advertise all that I offered. I used mostly word of mouth to advertise my business, and I discovered it was extremely powerful.

People are more likely to use a product or service that a friend or family member recommends. Because word of mouth is so powerful, it is important to always show up being your best for your business or your workspace. Take pride in what you do and deliver the greatest service possible so that your clients or customers will talk about their experience to their friends or family.

Word of mouth advertising can go the opposite way, too. Even if you haven't personally done business with a company, a bad review from a trusted friend will possibly discourage you from doing business with them.

Online reviews are held in the utmost importance today. Most of us will rely on the experience of others to make up our mind regarding making a purchase. It is sad when trolls knock down a business' rating and especially disappointing when they haven't even been to the business themselves. It is important to take all disappointing reviews with a grain of salt, and if it's your business they are critiquing, make any changes that are within your power to change.

Take a moment sometime to tune into the energy of online posts and platforms. Notice it is possible to sense if a person is angry and writing a rant or sending a hidden message to someone through a picture or a meme. Just go for a scroll and pick up what you are feeling as you read people's posts. There is so much energy coming at you in rapid pace that it is sometimes easy to get caught up in all the drama…and it's not even your drama!

Each platform has its own unique energy vibration. Facebook feels very gossipy and holds a 'need to know now' type of energy. It feels angry and a bit in-your-face. Most businesses use it for paid advertising and you are seeing fewer people posting personal life events. This doesn't mean it's not getting used. There are millions on it. Most people are just having a look around not being aware that they are being affected by the energy of others.

Could you imagine the world in which no one gets offended by different opinions online? Or a world in which we don't have to hear or see rants? The largest triggers I find online (and off) are politics, religion, and those darn vaccines! These three topics can start the greatest fights between the closest of friends. There is a lot of electrically charged energy between people with differing opinions on these topics. I'm sure you have experienced this also.

Instagram has a calmer energy than Facebook and it displays more beauty with pictures and less text. Even with calmer energy, there are still triggers and crazy posts.

Twitter feels to me that it is for the super busy (or people who think they are super busy). Limiting your characters and blurting out sentences of thought in rapid fire text seems to say, "Hurry up; next!"

LinkedIn is another platform that I have explored. It feels so serious and important. I do not connect with it, but do have a profile in case serious and important people need to find me.

Snapchat feels like a silly, playful platform. It feels like younger kids like to go on to play and connect. It has a very fun energy. When my nephew set me up, he expressed it was the greatest thing. At the time, I unfortunately did not connect well with it - delete. Possibly it was showing me that I needed more silly and playful energy in my life. Hmmm.

I'm sure there are other media platforms that hold other energy vibrations. What do you feel when you are on those sites? I guarantee it is different than your own personal email. Recently, a woman who I follow on social media talked about using email exclusively for her business, because it wasn't filled with all this crazy energy. You also own your email list and don't have to be afraid of a platform changing algorithms to mess up with your potential views. She makes a great point and yet, at the same time, may be missing out from the people who use social media. Just pay attention to how you feel when you use all platforms.

There are many people who take a social media cleanse. People do this because they are quite sensitive souls to energy and possibly feel they need a break from its intensity. Some know why they need to shut it off and some have no clue but just know that it makes them feel better. If you are being affected by worldwide energy, go on a social media fast for a day. Just a day! See what type of difference it makes in your life. You may love that feeling and crave more of it. Imagine all the extra time you will have when you don't have to respond to messages on your phone or check out what all your friends and so-called friends are doing. You may actually participate more in the present moment of your life!

Remember, you can monitor your social media accounts! You are in complete control and have the power to enjoy the people who are on your feed or you can simply delete them. Another option is to monitor what they see of your life and what you see in theirs. If this form of communication and essentially energy is bothersome for you, adjust your settings to make it as enjoyable of an experience as you can. (That's a good metaphor for all of life – adjust your settings!)

We have been consumed by this virtual life and people seem to have a harder time relating to the tangible world around them. If this is you, maybe it is time to come back to a simpler way of living. Possibly coming back to a life that involves face-to-face conversations or live phone conversations would be beneficial.

Maybe it's time to invite people to your home and have a rule to leave your phone in a bowl at the door so that you can have meaningful gatherings rather than someone always checking their phone. Or, maybe it's time to keep the phone in your pocket when out for dinner with your partner or friends so that you can look in their eyes and be interested in what they have to say. Would this energy exchange help or hinder our world? You can decide.

Thoughts to Ponder:

1. What social media sites do you use and how do you feel when you are using them?
2. Would it be a good idea in your life to go on a social media fast?
3. Are there people you need to delete or adjust your settings with?
4. What can you do to increase the connection of live relationships in your life?

CHAPTER 14

CLEARING SPACE

From time to time I travel to other communities to teach energy classes. Once, I taught in a beautiful new wellness centre. As I was given the tour, the man mentioned that there had been some funky energy in the space. Because most of the therapists felt it, the entire space was smudged. I loved how sensitive these people were to their space and knew this was going to be a super class because of it.

Smudging is a great way to clear a space, but is not always an ideal choice in a public building since many smudges can have a very strong smell (some smudges smell like marijuana) and sometimes a lot of smoke. This reminds me of a time when my friends smudged their classroom in a community college and the fire department had to be called after the alarm went off.

If you are energetically attracted to a particular smudge and you are able to smudge in your building, then go for it. Many people choose to smudge with sage, because it is an energetic cleanser. A lot of people use an abalone shell to hold the burning sage and an eagle's feather to move the smoke around. You can also smudge yourself, others, land, or buildings. Set your intention to purify and release negative energy from a person or space. You can intend to change the energy, increase the energy, or get rid of negative energy. Ask for help from your guides (God, Universe, Creator, etc.). If it's a home or business, talk to it as though it's a living person right in front of you. Ask for help, set the intention, and do the action trusting that it will be done.

If you are unable to smudge, your intention is just as powerful as a ritual ceremony. When your personal body and spirit vibration is high, you can move from room to room in a building stating your intention for the energy to clear and change and it will. You are powerful enough to not even need to be in the building. You can be miles away and state your commands for the energy to clear.

This may sound a bit farfetched, but you must try it to believe it. It really is no different than praying for a person who lives far away or doing distant Reiki on someone. We sometimes forget just how powerful we are and what our full potential is. Distant clearing of a space or a loved one is in your scope of possibilities, because you are energy!

Using the vibration of sound is also another way to clear energy in a space. To do this I use a handmade Native drum. My drum has my energy in it plus the energy of the moose that gifted its hide and the energy of the tree that makes up the frame. The vibration the drum makes is powerful and has been used many times to clear my own building. Singing bowls are also very popular and can help change the vibration of a space. Other forms of sound can also be used, including your voice.

Another way to clear energy is to use meditation. Meditation can be used for clearing a space, even if you are not in the space you are clearing. Below is a meditation you can do to clear a space and expand your energy field.

Connecting and Expanding Meditation

Choose a quiet spot where you won't be interrupted. Shut your phone off. Get comfortable and take some deep breaths as you begin to relax your body. Close your eyes and allow yourself to be here without judgment. Just breathe.

Place your hands on your heart. With your next exhale, imagine your heart's energy moving down your right leg into the earth below. As you inhale, imagine this energy returning to your heart's center through your left leg. Exhale through your right leg to the earth below and inhale back through your left leg to your heart. Be open to receive any contributions the earth would like to give you at this time. Take a few more breaths to receive as you loop this energy from the heart, through the body, to the earth, and back to the heart. You are connecting yourself to the ground and earth.

On your next inhale, imagine your heart energy moving up towards your head and into our galaxy. With your exhale, take your vision down to the head towards the heart. Inhale again towards the heavens, and exhale towards the heart. Continue this loop for a few breaths. Ask for any contributing energy that is needed in or around your body to be given to you. Take a few more breaths with this vision.

Now, let's connect these two loops. On your next inhale, imagine your heart energy moving up towards the heavens. Exhale the vision down the body through the heart, through the right leg and into the earth. Inhale up from the earth, through the left leg to the heart to the heavens. Exhale down from the heavens through the heart to the earth. Continue for a few more breaths with this vision, crossing the energy in the heart and breathing through the infinity symbol you created.

Bring your breath back to your heart. Imagine your loved

ones who fill you with joy and love. Feel that joy and love filling your heart. Take a few breaths feeling this energy.

With your next exhale, imagine this emotion filling your body. You may see a color or movement. Continue to breathe this love in and out expanding it past your body and into your energy field. With this vision of expansion, see your love energy filling the room.

Now imagine you are in your own workspace and that this love energy is filling the space. Imagine beautiful light flowing from you into your space. As you continue to breathe, imagine this light spreading into the building that you work in.

Ask that any negative residual energy from past clients, customers, and co-workers that is lingering in the building to be transformed into love and be used for the greater good of mankind. Intend that your workspaces be cleared of all residual and old energy. Affirm that any energy that is not serving a purpose for your highest good must leave. Imagine it being replaced with positive, calm, and productive energy. Fill your space with love and the vibration of gratitude and acceptance. Breathe this in for a few breaths and just stay with your awareness.

When you are ready, give thanks for all that has been given and shown. With your breath, come back to your current time and space in total allowance for all that is to come.

***

I used this meditation at a teacher's conference as we collectively cleared the energy in the buildings where they worked. Some of the schools were over 40 years old. Imagine the collective energy from past students and staff. We were not in each of the physical buildings; yet, we set the intention and felt the power as we cleared the lingering energy that was no longer serving a purpose.

This meditation grounds you to the earth's core and connects you to your higher power. The energy visualization crosses in the heart and forms an infinity symbol, reminding us that we each are infinite! We then expand love energy into our physical bodies and into our space, setting our intentions for what we desire.

Use and adapt this meditation however you feel called. The first part of the meditation gives you a quick way to ground yourself and feel connected. You can stop at that point or continue on.

Thoughts to Ponder:

1. Do you feel your home/workspace could use some attention and maybe a clearing?
2. When can you dedicate time to change the energy in these spaces?
3. What will your method be: smudge, sound, meditation, other?

4.   Do you notice any difference in your space when you use a meditation, smudge, or set your intentions for the energy to be cleared? By taking notice, this will develop your awareness for when a clearing is needed.

PART 3

THE ENERGY OF THE BODY

Feel the energy of your inner body. Immediately mental noise slows down or ceases. Feel it in your hands, your feet, your abdomen, your chest. Feel the life that you are, the life that animates the body. The body then becomes a doorway, so to speak, into a deeper sense of aliveness underneath the fluctuating emotions and underneath your thinking.

~ Eckhart Tolle

CHAPTER 15

THIS MARVELLOUS BODY

Have you ever wondered why we have a body? I believe we are a spirit having a human experience. If this belief is true, why were we given these physical bodies to house our spirit? Have you ever had these kinds of thoughts? (Or is it just me?)

I have wondered what the purpose of my body is for quite some time. I could have been created to just be a spirit without all this casing. Do I experience most of my existence in physical form? Maybe I chose to have this human experience, and maybe I even chose this body to house me? Have you ever felt stifled in your body or that your body is too small to contain your enormous spirit?

I know these are weird questions. Maybe this is what happens when a person works mostly in silence with massage clients; the brain starts to wonder. You will need to find your own truth in this since, of course, you do not have to believe what I believe.

Since we have these bodies, let's talk a bit about what they are capable of and possibly why we do have them. When I studied anatomy in massage college, I was blown away with the body's capabilities. Most of us have no idea what is going on automatically inside us. Even as you read this there are hundreds of functions happening. No one is telling the body to operate; it's just doing its thing. How and why does the body continue to stay alive?

What if it's the spirit that keeps the body alive and it's up to our human brains to keep the body charged? We recharge by self-care. I have always thought of sleep as a recharging station. Sleep is a mystery in itself. Why were we created to need sleep? Isn't it interesting how the world goes to sleep (for the most part) every night and wakes up to do life every morning? What happens when we are unconscious and dreaming? What is sleep's purpose? So many questions! Are you starting to see that I may have been a pain in the ass as a child? Maybe I still am as an adult. I was shut down a lot as a kid for asking too many questions the adults around me couldn't answer.

It's only been in the last 20 years that I have explored

some answers to these questions for myself. Here's the kicker: there are no concrete answers. It's just that simple. You must sift through all the information and form your own conclusions. It's a bit like navigating your way through Facebook. Everything is debated and, in the end, you must form your own opinion and truth.

Throughout the years, I have led many meditation classes. The first thing we tune into is our breath. Isn't it amazing how most creatures on the planet breathe? We could have evolved without the breath. Or could we have?

Breathing, as it has been shown to me, is the connection to all. On page 6 of Yoga Anatomy by Kaminoff and Matthew it states: "It is important to note that in spite of how it feels when you inhale, you do not actually pull air into the body. On the contrary, air is pushed into the body by the atmospheric pressure (14.7 pounds per square inch, or 1.03kg/cm^2) that always surrounds you. This means that the actual force that gets air into the lungs is outside of the body. The energy expended in breathing produces a shape change that lowers the pressure in the chest cavity and permits the air to be pushed into the body by the weight of the planet's atmosphere. In other words, you create the space, and the universe fills it."

What if breathing was our connection to All That Is? For anyone who does meditation or yoga, you know there is something magical to the breath. Yes, it keeps us alive and rejuvenates the body, but there is a bit more to it when you breathe deep and focus on it. Try it right now. Inhale deeply and hold your breath for a few counts. Exhale and push all air out of the lungs and diaphragm. You may even want to incorporate what I like to call baby breathing. If you are lucky enough to be around a baby or small child, just watch them breathe. They push their stomach out for the inhale and depress the stomach for the exhale. This is our normal natural breath.

Around age seven our life becomes more structured and we start to breathe shallower, from the upper portions of our lungs. A person who is under constant stress will breathe quite shallow, not allowing oxygen to flow through all parts of the body. Many people also hold their breath while they are thinking or when they perceive stressful events. This is very common and anyone who has been on my massage table has had their breathing checked out. I would say about half, if not more, are struggling to utilize their entire respiratory system, likely due to not being aware and by stress in their lives. This stress may have happened years ago and a new shallow breathing pattern may have been formed. I'm sure you have heard of the fight or flight system. Shallow breathing is one of the physiological responses to stress. Sometimes we are unable to reset this response by rest and it continues without awareness or attention.

An interesting point about the exhale is that it activates

the vagus nerve. The vagus nerve is the longest cranial nerve in the body and controls our parasympathetic nervous system. When this nerve is activated, heart rate decreases, muscles relax, vision restores, blood flows, and digestion normalizes. This helps decrease the symptoms of the fight or flight response. All this occurs just from exhaling.

What role does oxygen play in the body? This is just a small blurb from www.sharecare.com: "Oxygen is important to every cell in your body. ... Oxygen, through a process called oxidation, chemically changes food and liquid into energy. It's this "oxygen fire" that contracts our muscles, repairs our cells, feeds our brains, and even calms our nerves. Not only that, but breathing is our body's chief cleansing tool."

This mysterious atmospheric pressure pushes oxygen into our lungs so that we can make life saving chemical changes in our body in order to live another day. You likely have never even thought of this before. We are so mystical.

Thoughts to Ponder:

1.   Breathe and pay attention to your breath throughout the day. Is it shallow or calm, deep, and steady? Do you find yourself holding your breath? Just notice what is going on.
2.   Breathe even deeper. Practice some baby breaths by pushing the belly out on the inhale

and pulling the belly in on the exhale. Observe a baby if you have the chance. Let them teach you how to breathe.

3. Can you pinpoint a time in your life when stress may have changed your breathing? Are you stuck in that moment? Sometimes awareness is enough to move a body forward, and in this case, help the body to breathe with more ease.

CHAPTER 16

ENERGY AND THE BODY

Studying energy and the body is probably one of my favourite things to explore. I work with this every single day in my practice and I love and respect what the body has to say. Most people never think of their body as a messenger, but it is very vocal and wants to show you more of who you are and how to help yourself. Through my studies, I have wondered if this could possibly be the reason why we have a body. The body speaks. Can we gain enlightenment by listening to it?

This subject feels like my lifelong work, and why I came to the planet. Even as I look back on how everything in my life lined up to study massage, then energy, meditation, and, more recently, medical intuition, I see that it was all planned out. I was open to playing the leading role in the play that was already written - the play of my life.

Intuitive communication first started showing up in my massage practice many years ago. One day in particular, a client came in after having seen most of the practitioners in our office. She was complaining of headaches. I did the usual massage routine of upper back, neck, pectorals, head, and face, and started to pick up more on her body.

Her body was sad. It felt to me that she was going through a heartache in her life. The body was mourning and the left shoulder was actually internally rotating towards her heart in a protective posture. It appeared that this was what was holding her head in a forward posture probably causing extra stress on the back of the head and leading to the perpetual headaches that were unexplained by her medical doctor and other health providers. (Side note: When a medical provider cannot diagnose a problem, but the client feels something is not right, this is almost always energy/emotional related.)

I ignored this message, because this was out of my scope of practice as a massage therapist. Besides, there was no proof that what I was sensing was true. I finished the massage, gave her the typical stretches, and had my hand on the door when she said, "Is there anything else you can tell me about my body?"

I have thought of this simple question years later because

it literally changed the course of my career. "Yes!" I said. The opening of possibility was cracked and I chose to step through.

I started by saying that this was not in my scope of practice, then told her what I was feeling her body was trying to communicate with her. She started bawling. It was all relating. The connection was made between her emotions and her body and what the symptoms were actually saying beyond a physical diagnosis. (That is the exact definition of Medical Intuition, by the way.)

This client had been abused by her husband, and they were now separated. Her life was basically turned upside down. She mourned him even though she hated him, and she grieved her marriage. All of this was held in the heart chakra's energy center. It made sense to her why her body was in a protective stance. She was scared of being hurt, and she was still licking her wounds from all she had gone through.

I stayed with her as she caught her breath. I really didn't have much to coach her through, because sometimes just having the awareness of the issue will start the process of resolution. Sometimes just holding space for someone to express emotion from their body is all that is required. I am also not a marriage/divorce coach. I do have my own experiences and I do respect that everyone heals in their own time. I believed my job of relaying the message was done. It was now her job to find help and start the physical and emotional healing.

I remember feeling elated after that appointment. It was incredibly rewarding. I felt like I was making a difference in someone's life. It was even more rewarding than just a massage. I found the root pain that was causing the body to respond. I knew instantly that this was what I wanted to do with the rest of my career.

I flipped through my mind's rolodex and tried to think of someone who could teach me more. I remembered a lady who taught Medical Intuition and I enrolled in her classes that week. It's crazy how fast things happen when you are ready!

Through this training I learned how to hone my own intuition. Everyone has intuition, and it really is our superpower. I wanted to use mine in my everyday life and to enhance my career as a massage therapist.

Today, I combine my teachings, gifts, and experience to give a person the best of all worlds. The body wants to be heard, but many have forgotten its language. Our lives get so full and noisy that we cannot hear the body's subtle messages. Even when the body turns up the volume, we ignore it or we are quick to medicate it. Have you ever noticed this when you feel a cold coming on? What would happen if you stopped what you were doing, found some superfoods, hydrated your body, and went straight to bed? Likely, you'd wake up and the cold would be gone.

If you are like most people, you may take a cough drop and keep going. Then, your nose begins to run and your throat feels sore. You go find something at the drug store to keep you going. You are exhausted, but you must keep going because the world will stop if you do, right? Maybe caffeine and energy drinks get you through the day.

Then, the cold knocks you on your ass and you cannot move. Everything aches. You lose your voice, and you look like hell. Now, you are forced to stay home. There are some of you that will medicate even more just to keep going, all the while possibly infecting those around you and creating extra work for your body to process all the medications. The body is trying to get your attention. Quit numbing it.

I can't tell you how many people I have come across who have told me that they do not have time to be sick. They go to work sick, circulating their sickness to their co-workers. Really, they are just increasing the time it will take for them to get well. Some clients have even told me that they cannot take a sick day, because they may need them in the future. Umm, sick days are for when you are sick. Take them and restore yourself.

When the body is sick, it's trying to get your attention. Isn't it time to stop overriding it with your thoughts and medications? The poor body. It's only trying to be a messenger. You think your dog is loyal to you – this body is much more loyal, but can really only take so much. It's your job to start a conversation with your body and listen to what it tells you. It's your job to take care of you!

Thoughts to Ponder:

1. Tune in to your body at this moment and feel its entirety. Where is it holding tension? Now ask that tension what it would like to tell you. Stay quiet, and just listen. Spend some time with this and develop a daily habit of checking in.

2. Do you have a mysterious symptom or physical issue that western medicine is unable to diagnose or help? You may want to hire a Medical Intuitive to help you understand what is going on.

CHAPTER 17

CHAKRA ENERGY

Most people on the planet have heard of the word chakra (pronounced shaw cra or chuk raw). This word has been around for a while. If you haven't heard of chakras, just do some googling. You will find many different thoughts and beliefs about them.

With most alternative medicine, there is little to no scientific evidence that chakras even exist. In fact, there is no unified theory about chakras (similar to most things in life); therefore, you will need to find what feels good to you and what resonates with your own truth.

It is said (from the world wide web) that the chakra system was first used in India between 1500 and 500 BC as documented in the oldest text called the Vedas.

Chakras are said to be wheel-like energy centers within the body which can relate to emotions, body parts, organs, colors, sounds, foods, gemstones, and more. They are quite fascinating. I have found the information that they provide very useful while balancing a person's mind and body.

In the early 2000's, I began to teach Reiki. There is a section in the first-degree manual about chakras. For most my students at that time, it was the first time they had even heard the term. In the classroom settings today, we mostly just review the section since most students now know more about chakras than the manual provides. It has been an interesting shift to watch.

Why are these energy centers important? We will take a look at each chakra in the following chapters. I will not repeat the basic information that you can find on the Internet, but rather touch on how the mind and body along with the emotions are held in each chakra and how we can work with this information.

Most people can agree on the seven basic chakras. In the following chapters, we will look at what I feel as a therapist when working on someone. Something that may be controversial with other chakra healers is that I believe there is no simple way to heal a chakra. What I mean by that is the chakra does not simply heal by putting a crystal on it or visualizing a color and a ball spinning.

Sometimes in my healing practice I say that it's not the lack of Tylenol that has caused your headache, meaning "Let's get to the root issue, instead of covering it up, so that it won't reappear in the future." It's the same with the chakras. It is not the lack of a crystal or the vibration that the crystal provides, or a lack of a visualization that has kept the chakra unhealthy or unbalanced. That is some of it, but there is much more to it. The key is found in what the chakra represents in the body, mind, emotions, history, and even past life history of the person.

In the next few chapters, we will take a look at the beautiful gift the chakras are to our bodies and see what they have to reveal to us.

Thoughts to Ponder:

Take a moment to familiarize yourself with the chart on the following page for the locations of the main seven chakras. Knowing their location and what they are called will help you understand the following chapters.

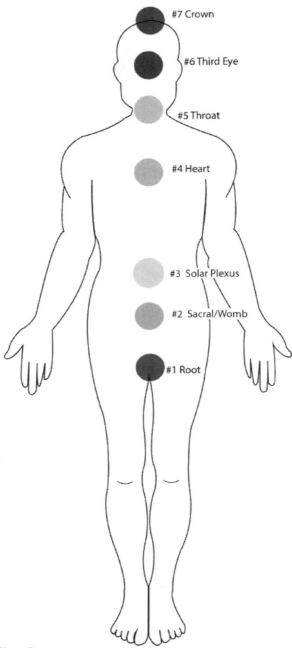

Chart credit: Kerris Dancy

CHAPTER 18

CHAKRA #1 – THE ROOT CHAKRA

The root chakra is in the area of the pubic bone or, if we were to have a tail, at the coccyx area of the spine. Ok, I just have to say it - have you ever wondered why we don't have tails? I wonder what we would do with them if we had them?

The first chakra basically encompasses the hips, legs, feet, and the base of our spine. This area develops in humans from the time we are a fetus until approximately age seven. Different sources refer to other ages, but this seems to be the most common thought. The age is the important piece of information, because so much happens in our formative years - probably more than we will ever know.

In some cases, our parents possibly didn't want us or were overwhelmed with the pregnancy. They likely wouldn't tell you that today, but it is possible you may have experienced abandonment issues before you were even born. It may sound ludicrous, but think of all the studies that have been done that tell us the fetus can recognize a parent's voice. You don't think a fetus can pick up energy? It can.

Ages one through seven are the forming years when we are basically told what to do and how to do it. We accept another's way (parent's/guardian's) as the truth to our world. We rely on others to keep us alive and provide the basics that we need to survive. Sometimes, parents do a terrible job and don't even realize how their own horrible upbringing will influence their child's life. They think their children are just toddlers and things won't affect them. They do. Upbringing affects your energy. The root chakra is the chakra that holds it all.

One of my own experiences in this area was remembering an event that really doesn't seem that traumatic, but had a significant effect on my energy. I was about four years old and fell asleep in the living room of our new home. My grandparents lived less than a block away and my mom needed to return something to my grandma. She left the house thinking she would be back before I woke up. She was wrong. I awoke to no one around and started to cry. I felt abandoned. My mom returned, held me to soothe me, then she laughed and said, "Did you really think I would leave you?" Ummmm, well...you kinda did!

I was made out to be wrong, and I retreated as a person that day. My little brain was sure I was right, but something didn't make sense. My mom was the caretaker, and in my world at the age of four, she was right...all the time! Later in life, I remember not participating in questions being asked in the classroom, because I was scared of being wrong. I had held onto this feeling of being wrong until I recently recognized it while doing my own inner work.

Even the smallest events can leave a mark on our psyche. The larger, more traumatic events do too, and, if left unresolved, often develop into physical conditions.

A few weeks ago, a beautiful woman came to see me. She was in the middle of cancer treatments. She had been diagnosed with cervical cancer even though she had a hysterectomy. Advanced imaging revealed cancer in her iliopsoas muscle.

She was ready for new ideas to complement western medicine. We talked a lot and I told her my ways in healing, which is to find the root and then change the energy in whatever ways we can to manipulate the condition. I use a few tools, but Reiki, visualizations, and medical intuition are my main modalities along with listening to the energy of the body and what it wants to say.

As we started to work, I had my hands on her hips (first chakra). I asked what had happened when she was a child, and if she had a difficult upbringing. I always respect when someone does not want to share their journey, but that was why she was on my table.

Her story began. A family member had sexually abused this woman when she was very young. No one knew, and to this day, only her husband and maybe a handful of close friends had heard her story. She kept it all inside of her for various reasons. She held no ill will towards her family. I'm sure a flood of emotions overtook her throughout her life and even now as she shared one of her deepest secrets. The biggest thing I noticed was that she carried this all on her own and kept that energy inside her body. The energy likely became congested and the cells likely began to stick together to form the cancer within the energy center of the first chakra. Crazy? Yes! This is the way the body works!

Even more crazy was that she no longer had a cervix because of the hysterectomy. The congested energy was still there and resided in the root chakra. The cancer cells found a new home, which she told me had less than a 1% chance of taking root in the iliopsoas muscle. It doesn't make any sense to develop cancer in this muscle if you look at it from a western medicine standpoint. From an energetic view, it makes complete sense.

In her entire lifetime, she never knew how to get this

congested energy out of her body. We talked about sharing this secret with her family. There likely would be massive healing with an honest conversation, not out of hatred or spite, but to heal the body and free it from this covered up secret.

The other aspect of this story is that her parents/guardians failed to protect her from abuse. I say failed but, really, can you fail if you do not know? When you have a child's brain, yes. A child wants and needs protection from their guardians. When that is not given (even if they didn't know what was going on), trauma is created that needs to be healed. Once a person walks through it (rather than around it), healing can be initiated. When we ignore it, it will keep appearing in our life and give us more chances to come face-to-face with it for healing.

The body, in its brilliance, wants to get the energy out. It's trying to get your attention first by pain and discomfort, and then it talks louder with a condition or a disease. It is up to us to either figure it out or find someone to interpret what is going on.

I am so proud of this client who chose to include energy medicine alongside the western medical system. She worked hard on expressing her emotions through various techniques. She visualized the tumours shrinking and disappearing. We shook up the energy with Reiki, sound healing, and the breath. Prior to printing this book, this client reported to me that she was 99% cancer free. Astonishingly, the tumours disappeared, and she, along with her family, was left in joyous shock.

We spoke after this miracle that we prayed for, and discussed why we go into shock when our body spontaneously heals. We believed she got to the root of her dis-ease and that is what helped cure her. Why do we think this is just for a select few? We all have this power within us. We must believe it.

In Chapter 2, I mentioned the story of how I found Reiki because of my itchy legs. The message that was interpreted from my body was that I needed to put my roots down in England or go back to Canada. This energy resided in the first chakra. This makes sense because the first chakra represents foundation, stability, home life, and our basic needs. It is where we put roots down figuratively and literally.

The root chakra holds many clues as to what may be happening in the body and, of course, we all seem to have some stuff to observe from our upbringing. The legs are the pillars of life and can support you or can crumble beneath you. The knees represent how flexible you are with change or how adaptable you may be to stress. The hips represent moving forward in decisions and life in general. I see them as a locomotive train type of action.

We often have an idea of what we want to do in life. It's a very quick thought and we may second guess it.

Intuition happens in a split second, then our brain takes over, usually ruining the idea because it wants to analyze it to death. We then move into a push-pull type of energy as our spirit wants to do one thing, and our mind another. We fight it. This energy often gets stuck in the hips. Fear is what keeps us back and includes fear of the unknown, fear of being wrong, fear of what others will say, fear of failing, and fear of rejection. It happens to all of us.

I had a counsellor that I saw for a year after my divorce. She would always play this game with me. I would give her my problem and excuses and she would say, "What's the worst that could happen?" I'd tell her my worst-case scenario (My parents will be mad at me; my parents will disown me; I will be left alone) and she would keep asking, "Okay, and then what's the worst that could happen?" We would eventually get to where the answer would be death. Today, because I believe we are spirits in a body and this body will eventually die, I am not afraid of the worst-case scenario. Many people are afraid of death. If you are one of these people, you will want to come to terms with what you believe in order to understand what this counsellor was trying to get at. The point is to find what really is the worst-case scenario if you spoke your truth and stopped making excuses.

These fears play a part in everyone's life. Have you ever thought about what would happen if you actually succeeded? What if you spoke your truth? What if the idea in your mind came true? What if it brought you a ton of joy and freedom? You will never find out if you do not attach ACTION to it.

So, do it! It's time to start living the life you came to Earth to live. If it scares you, it's likely what you are supposed to do and, often times, that fear is the soul's excitement.

Note: The general intuitive insights about how the body responds do not necessarily apply to all people. It is best to have a personal assessment from a medical intuitive or an energy therapist who offers insights by tapping into your own unique energy.

Thoughts to Ponder:

1. In your childhood, were there times while growing up that you felt rejected or abandoned, or had not had your basic needs taken care of? Are you ready to start exploring those? (It's okay if you need professional help to uncover more of what is possibly holding you back).

2. Is there discomfort in the lower part of your body that needs to be acknowledged or requires professional help?

3. Are you pondering a dream or wanting to make a move in life that your mind may be talking you out of?

CHAPTER 19

CHAKRA #2 – THE SACRAL CHAKRA

The sacral chakra is located just below your belly button. It develops between ages seven and fourteen. Its most common theme is self-identity which makes a lot of sense considering the age bracket that it is related to. These ages are also the forming years of your life. Our personality starts to shine and we realize what we like and dislike. This is also where we become more structured, have less playtime, and take our life more seriously.

Some kids at this age start doing more parental duties if they have younger siblings or have a parent who is delegating more than they should. Some of us become the parent and look after our own parents. The identity of caregiver usually builds into caring for others more than ourselves later on in life. This type of identity is very common among women who did not have a caregiver/ mother who looked after her own self. As kids, we mimic what our parent is doing.

When this chakra is out of balance, we see physical conditions in the reproductive and digestive areas. Have you ever experienced stomach pain for no apparent reason? What about difficulty in conceiving? Or possibly in eliminating? These are some common issues that arise when this chakra needs attention. Wouldn't it be cool to have a chakra doctor? "I will now examine your second chakra." I guess, in a sense, that is what energy workers do.

Think about all the sensitivities in our world today. I sure didn't have that growing up in the 70's and 80's. Today, there are so many things you cannot even put in your child's lunch because it may kill another child! One other observation is how many women need to use in vitro to conceive. As I am writing this, I can think of four people in my own life who have had to use in vitro treatments.

What does this chakra want to say? What are we missing that is possibly leading to the physical complications? What do we need to know about our identity?

Again, we will all have different messages. These are

general observations from hundreds of clients. The most important message here is to take a look at how we self-identify. How do you see yourself? Is this something that you have even thought about? Who are you?

It's deep, but these are questions that can help the flow of energy in this part of the body. When energy is flowing, the physical symptoms have a better chance of disappearing, because the root problem will have been addressed.

If your best friends had to describe you, what adjectives would they use? If you had to describe yourself, and weren't allowed to use labels (wife, mother, business owner, etc.) what would you say?

I have a childhood friend who came to me one day and was out of sorts because someone had offered to purchase her business. This isn't such an easy thing in our little town and I was happy for her. She wasn't as excited as I was. When I questioned her on this, we discovered that her identity was in the business. This business was where she processed a lot of her hardships, gained friendships, and motivated and encouraged others. This business shaped her into who she was and she was unsure if she would know herself without it.

This is a very common thing with business, parenthood, and any position in our work place. We think that it is who we are when, really, it is just what we do. Without my friend's knowledge, I posted on Facebook that if you know this person, could you tell her who she is without her labels. Many cool descriptions came in including that she was smart, humorous, loving, kind, generous, encouraging, and so on. I typed up the summary and sent it to her with the message of, "If you ever forget who you are, this is it. This is more you than being a mother (that is something you do), or a wife (a term for a relationship) or a chef (a profession)."

Who are you, really?

We identify to roles in life because that's what the majority of people do. No one has ever shown us that we are something different. When we are in the ages of 7-14, we are trying to figure out who we are, but the adults around us (parents, guardians, coaches, pastors, etc.) are all telling us what to do and who to be. It's no wonder we get confused. It's time to start realizing how much of your identity has been formed by other people's ideas of who you are and how you should act, and recognize that maybe that really isn't who you are.

In meditation, we always start with our breath and taking deep inhales and exhales to start being present. It is interesting to me that shallow breathing starts in the age of the second chakra when we first (usually) perceive stress. I believe this stress is from not being able to truly be ourselves. Instead, we are expected to be someone who someone else wants us to be. We follow along so that we can identify with the tribe that is raising us. We are told what to do and how to do it and, in turn, that shapes us.

If you have never taken a look at this for yourself and possibly suffer from physical symptoms in the lower abdominal area, then what are you waiting for? It's time to be all that you are meant to be, because you are here to be authentically you! No labels, just you!

Thoughts to Ponder:

1. Do you experience physical conditions in the second chakra area?
2. Who are you without your labels?
3. Who influenced you as a child?
4. Are you living your authentic truth?
5. How has your upbringing helped you identify? Is it your truth?

CHAPTER 20

CHAKRA #3 – THE SOLAR PLEXUS CHAKRA

The solar plexus chakra is located above the belly button. This energy center develops from our teenage years well into our twenties. For me, this was my least favourite time as I was trying to figure out who I was and my place in this world.

Similar to the sacral chakra, the solar plexus chakra has a lot to do with who we are and how we see ourselves. Our upbringing and our circumstances all affect the first three chakras.

The solar plexus has to do with power, in particular, self-power. It is responsible for self-esteem, self-worth, and belief in our abilities. It also is the self-love center. How do you really feel about yourself? All those thoughts and beliefs reside here.

The organs in this area include the intestines, liver, gall bladder, lower lungs, diaphragm and middle to lower back. It comes as no surprise to me that a lot of us carry extra weight in the second and third chakras, possibly a protection from being hurt by others.

Again, this is a part of life that no one really teaches us. Did we ever learn self-esteem and self-worth? Whoever showed us how to love ourselves? Likely, your parents were too busy making a living and making sure everyone survived. Our parents did the best they knew how and now it's time to learn how to do even better. It is time!

Self-esteem is really how you view your self-identity. To me, it is built by doing something really great and getting praised for it. Our esteem rises and we strive for more. What happens if you are not really that great at anything? Or, what happens if you have no one in your life to encourage you? Possibly, others don't even know the importance of that encouragement, or maybe they are jealous of you. Your self-esteem suffers. When that happens, energy can get stuck here in the third chakra. You many even have a close relationship with someone in your life who just doesn't say anything, good or bad, about your achievements. This feeling of neglect becomes congested in the solar plexus.

Self-worth is knowing that you are just as worthy of everything in life as the next person. I know adults who do not believe this for themselves, and therefore, are unable to build self-worth in their own children. Even some teachers and clergy do not have the belief we are equal, but rather there is a hierarchy in life. Your worthiness suffers greatly with these old, out-dated, small-minded beliefs.

If this describes you and your upbringing, you may want to seriously ponder, "Who am I?" Eckhart Tolle says when you ask this question enough, eventually you will get to the point where you say, "I am That", meaning, "I am everything." When you can believe this, you will start to believe in your worth and that there is no difference between you and me, or you and Oprah. We are all the same and worthy of everything.

I can't imagine what some of the minority ethnic groups have gone through in this area, because of the discrimination they have faced for many generations. In my community there are a lot of First Nations people. The suffering they have felt from policies of assimilation and the stupid belief that we are all not equals is insane. The Residential Schools, that were finally dismantled only in the 1990's, were set up to make these people more 'white'. Have you heard of anything more stupid and hurtful?

Being different does not make us less than. Embrace your differences. The world would be such a boring place if we were all the same. We all have so much to offer just by being who we are.

When people are hurt and thought of as second class, it is no wonder that they grab anything that will make them numb. We numb in many ways, but most of us think of numbing with food, drinks, drugs, or alcohol. It is interesting to note that all of these are processed in the liver, which resides in the third chakra. There is a huge connection with self-worth, addictions, and the third chakra.

Another interesting note is that when we are under stress, we breathe very shallow. The diaphragm is rarely engaged in most peoples' breathing. Fear of not being good enough, being ridiculed, or laughed at has a way of sucking the life out of us and depleting our breathing patterns. Feeling less than also depletes our breathing capacities. Chronic stress does as well. These are all third chakra issues.

Self-love is probably our greatest battle and, when reached, our greatest victory. It is a lifelong learning journey to loving ourselves. Some think it is selfish to take care of ourselves first before others. For some of you, this will be a hard concept to swallow. We have been taught that others are more important. We have been taught to think of others first, and to help out our brother before ourself. Are these statements still true for you?

Even the airlines have it right – "Put your mask on first before you help anyone else." Why do they request that? What help are you to others when you cannot even help yourself? It's the same for all parts of life. Too many of us are racing around helping every organization and every person we love. Our own cup is so empty that we are really just filling space and trying to help from depletion. We crash, but keep going thinking others are unable to function without us. Am I speaking to you?

I had a client that cancelled her massage appointment because she was feeling sick, but ended up going to work because they needed her. I have another client who has been fighting a cold for a month or two but doesn't have time to take off work because they need her. (Hint: colds and flus should not last for months). Another client will not take time off work even though she is sick because she wants to save her sick days for when she needs them. (That would be today.) Hello!!!! Are you listening to this? How do we help others when we cannot even help ourselves?

You are #1 in your life. Take care of yourself as if you are #1. If you cannot think this way yet, just take a moment to ponder what you are teaching your children, because they are watching and learning, and could use self-care tips when they leave home.

When I first started dating my husband, he said to me, "Who do you love the most in your life, top 10?" I remember saying, "Well, God, you, my family, friends, co-workers." He laughed and said, "Where are you? You didn't even make your own list!" That was 20 years ago. I am now #1 on my list, and you should be too!

I hope you are getting the underlying theme of just how important you are, how worthy you are, and how equal you are to everyone. Imagine a world where everyone thinks like this in a balanced way.

Being out of balance in the solar plexus chakra would be a person who comes across as arrogant and greedy. This type of energy presents by someone thinking they are the best and everyone else is less than. Healthy self-esteem balance is the key to a healthy third chakra.

If you cannot believe in yourself enough to know that you are equal to all humanity and worthy of love, respect, and kindness, then you must find your tribe to help raise you up until you do believe this. I speak of this tribe often. It is an important piece of life. In no way is that one word meant to offend any particular group of people. Finding people who have done some work on themselves and can relate to where you are at is incredibly valuable. They never tell you how to be. They just encourage you and allow for where you are in your journey.

As you grow and open yourself up to your awareness, you may find that some people fall away from your life, and your circle will become much smaller. One day, you may not need as many influences in your life. Rather, you'll enjoy your own company with your own spirit. Finding this part of you can be the greatest excitement and fulfillment of your life. Your tribe will keep you in check and help you connect to all that you are.

Thoughts to Ponder:

1. On a scale of 1-10 (10 being healthy and strong) where would you rate your self-esteem?
2. On a scale of 1-10 (10 being healthy and strong) where would you rate your self-worth?
3. Who or what has helped you develop self-esteem and self-worth in your life?
4. Who or what has led to the depletion of self-esteem and self-worth in your life?
5. Who do you want in your tribe?

CHAPTER 21

CHAKRA #4 – THE HEART CHAKRA

The fourth chakra is also known as the heart chakra. It is located in the center of the chest where the heart is. This chakra is really why I started studying the mind/body connection. It holds a great deal of information and affects everyone. There is no age attached to its learning.

This chakra connects the lower and upper energy centers (chakras). The lower chakras are all about our physical presence and how we perceive ourselves based on our upbringing and the influences we had growing up. The upper chakras are all based on our expression of what we know to be true plus our connection to our higher self and guides. The heart connects the upper and lower chakras together.

The heart chakra carries issues from our physical upbringing as well as deeper unexplained emotions and love. Everything is found in this area. The major organ, of course, is the heart. This chakra also includes the breasts, shoulders, arms, hands, upper lungs, thymus gland, mid-to-upper back, and ribs.

The entire human race is presenting with more rounded shoulders and is humped over in this area due to the lovely electronic devices that have taken over our world. Not only have they taken over our ways to communicate, but also our ability to connect with other humans. Have you ever talked to a teenager or tried to hire them for a job? They are sometimes unable to make eye contact; they answer in short sentences (if they even form them); and, they sit in a chair in a slump as though a device was in front of them. This is really scary for mankind, physically and mentally. I'm not saying it's everyone, but it is present in kids and even adults these days.

A lot of my business friends report that when you hire and discipline a millennial or try to show them another way, their heart center is so underdeveloped that their feelings become severely hurt. They end up quitting without the ability to communicate why. Is this what our devices are doing?

Do you limit your screen time with your kids? Have you engaged in their life to show them things that are more

fun than staring at their screen for hours at a time?
Maybe you do the same thing?

What does this have to do with the fourth chakra? The
heart chakra is all about love, connection, joy, nurturance,
and emotional pain including mourning, grieving,
loneliness, and depression. These are emotions connected
to physical contact with others, meaning there is an
exchange. There is no or very little emotional exchange
with devices. A child or teen needs physical exchanges
with their parents, friends, and pets to experience what it
means to be human. A computer exchange will never
provide them the value of emotional interaction or teach
them that it's okay to be sad and grieve the loss of a
grandparent. A computer exchange will not be able to
hug and nurture them to a place where they know it's
going to be okay and that they are okay.

Computers do provide a purpose for many things, but are
useless when it comes to providing emotional nurturing
and development.

Issues with the heart chakra come up a lot with my
clients. A few months ago, a friend of mine, Jen, (who is
a yoga teacher), and I put together a yoga chakra class.
She introduced the poses to help balance the seven major
energy centers, and I did intuitive reads on each
participant as to which chakra needed attention and why.
Before class she asked me, "Which chakras keep coming
up as needing the most attention?" Surprisingly (or not),

chakras 1, 4 and 5 were very common with the group of 12 we worked with. I have a feeling that if taken through a larger test group, the result would be the same. The first chakra, the root, is the foundation of your life. The fourth, the heart, is how you process your emotions of love; and the fifth, the throat, is how you express yourself. Every chakra has its purpose, but these three tend to stand out when we are facing our crises in life.

As I mentioned, my introduction to medical intuition was through a client having issues in her heart chakra. Many others have come through my door and expressed this imbalance too. One huge issue that I feel needs to be addressed, because of its frequency, is breast cancer. There have been so many people in my life, and I am sure in yours, that have had this diagnosis. Breast cancer is a heart chakra issue. I will speak about the messages of the heart chakra with regards to it, but just note that I am not diagnosing or prescribing treatment. (This goes for anything I speak of).

Breast cancer is, of course, in the breast tissue (fourth chakra), and is defined as a mass of cellular growth. This is very dense tissue. When a chakra is out of balance, there is usually either a lack of or an abundance of energy in the area. If this continues for a long period of time, it can start to affect the physical body. This isn't a new theory. If you study mind/body connection, this is a common thread that is gaining a lot of attention in the medical communities.

Many people believe that breast cancer and many cancers are genetic. The debate is on and I'm not advocating one way or the other. I would just like to present a different thought on the matter. If no one in your ancestral line broke the belief or took action to heal the emotions held in the fourth chakra, then is it possible that the environment may have set the body up to express cancer? Can emotions cause cancer, not only breast cancer, but all cancers?

Years ago, a beautiful woman brought her son who was dying of cancer to see me. I would do whatever he allowed as far as massage and energy work to enhance his quality of life. He eventually passed away, and I know her soul was ripped. Most of us will never be able to relate to the pain of losing a child. Years later, she unfortunately developed breast cancer. We talked about the deep hurt she endured with the loss of her son's life, and if this possibly contributed to her body's response. She thought it may be possible, yet, how does a body not respond as hers did? Deep loss and hurt, love from the heart, mourning and grieving all reside in the heart. How do we express these emotions? That's a great question and we will address it further in the next chapter.

Another acquaintance of mine has had two rounds of cancer. She is not as open to talk about her emotional state and other factors besides genetics and treatment. That's ok, to each their own. I do know that she grew up in a generation where no one talked about their feelings or expressed them. The mothers of those days also did not know how to emotionally nurture their children as no one had taught them that, either. (This is a huge factor in fourth chakra health). Is it possible that her body responded to the lack and longing of emotional connection here?

One more client of mine was recently diagnosed with breast cancer and is undergoing treatment. She is a lovely woman and, when she comes in, she is always in a hurry. She runs with her kids from event to event, to tournaments in different cities, here and there. She has basically told me she doesn't have time to slow down. I was so proud of her to receive regular massage as this was likely one of the only times she nurtured herself. Could cancer develop from the lack of self-love and self-nurturance? Is it possible it is the body's way to get our attention to take even better care of ourselves?

A final example of discomfort in this area was of a client who complained of shoulder pain. When shoulder pain is in both shoulders and not from trauma, there is usually an energy connection. She had been caring for her mom for the last few months before her mom's passing. She was exhausted and her body was starting to tell her to stop and rest. Her shoulders were tight and painful. She energetically carried her mom to her deathbed and had taken on tons of responsibility.

Extreme self-care is required when the fourth chakra is

grieving. It is all a recipe for disaster if not attended to.

The fourth chakra is an important one, because it connects heavily with self-love and self-care (the themes of this book). Who do you love the most in this world? Imagine treating yourself with the exact same kindness and compassion as you would this person, and then multiply it by 1000. That is the recipe for self-love...and a healthy fourth chakra.

Thoughts to Ponder:

1. How are you nurturing the relationships around you?
2. How are you nurturing the relationship you have with yourself?
3. Where in your life can you love yourself even greater?

CHAPTER 22

CHAKRA #5 – THE THROAT CHAKRA

The throat chakra is located in the throat area. It includes the neck, thyroid, mouth, esophagus, tongue, trachea, larynx, and all tissues in this area. This is a very common area to have an imbalance of energy since most of us were not taught its most dominant theme: speaking your truth.

I remember as a child that I had croup. My mom would always wrap me in a blanket and take me outside to breathe. Imagine a small child waking you up at night (somehow it always happened at night) and telling you she can't breathe. Scary! Croup is inflammation around the vocal cords and windpipe. While I don't understand why it occurred as a baby other than carrying over energy from another lifetime, or possibly carrying the energy of my parents through the womb, I do understand why it kept reoccurring into my 20's.

The throat chakra is responsible for expressing your emotions, mostly in the form of speech, but can also be in the form of creativity. As a child, I conformed to the ways of my parents and grandparents as most of us do. My aunt told me that I was always questioning why we did what we did. My questions were often ignored and a lot of them were unable to be answered. For example, how was it possible that there was life before Christ if he made the earth and it started at zero? I'm sure I was a joy to have around, like I still am! If we never question things, we never have a chance to find our own truth.

One thing I learned later was that my truth didn't have to be the same as my family's truth. Whew! Once I made this connection, my throat has never produced croup again.

My last episode of croup was in my early 20's. It's really not a fun condition. As an adult I was sitting outside trying to breathe, calm myself down, and not panic. I don't think I even took any medication for it. I certainly didn't know at that time what kind of emotional connection the fifth chakra played in it. I was in my first marriage and unable to speak my truth. I didn't even have my own truth yet. I hid behind my husband's truth and, well, that wasn't working for me. My body, as brilliant as it always is, was looking out for me and trying to get my attention.

Since the topic of speaking your truth and expressing your emotions kept coming up in my practice, I decided to create a class called "5 Strategies to Express Negative Emotions". I was following a speaker online who told me to do a free class and then pitch my services at the end. I was hoping to gain some medical intuitive clients. I advertised the class and had 32 people registered. This would fill all the chairs I could find in our office. I was super excited that people wanted to hear how to easily do this. "Heck, I may even get a client out of it!" I thought.

The day arrived and I patiently waited for people to gather. Seven people showed up. Seven!!!! I had turned people away because I didn't have room. Seven. Now imagine starting a class on expressing negative emotions when you are fuming inside and need to do some expressing of your own!

After some deep breathing and positive mental self-talk, I began to teach the class. It actually became comical in my mind as I moved through the material. I realized I was the one who was being taught through this experience.

The greatest lesson for me that day was that fair exchange needed to be given, any exchange really. It didn't have to be money. The energy exchange engages the 'giver' into participating with their own healing and lessons.

Because we are talking about fifth chakra energy and expressing ourselves, I will leave you with my top five ways to get this energy out of your body so that it does not become dense and cause physical conditions.

1.   Have a Conversation

This is only applicable if the person is alive, willing, and you are not too explosive.

This is one of the most freeing things you can do for yourself. YES, this action and your life are all about you and not them. It is about giving you the power back in your own life. What you need to do is schedule a time to talk. The talk needs to be about you expressing how you felt by what was said, and if there were any unsaid things to add. It is possible that no solution is going to be made by this discussion.

It is not our responsibility in life to make a person act the way we think they should or say the things we think they should say. It is our responsibility to express our feelings. That is all. You may need to agree to disagree. I guarantee that once you are able to express your feelings, the trigger of anger, hatred, frustration, and irritation will be less or completely dissolved.

When done face-to-face, you have a greater chance of

resolving the issue, because sometimes the person has come to an understanding about how they may have hurt you. Texts, emails, and anything less than face-to-face can get relayed in the wrong way. It is amazing to me how many very important messages are being communicated in this way.

Tip: never attack a person personally. It's just cruel and unnecessary. You are speaking for you in order to let the energy out of your body. This allows for greater things to occupy its space rather than frustration and worry.

Know that you may lose the friendship/relationship. They may have lots to say that you will like or dislike, but just remember, you are expressing yourself and the outcome does not matter. You are helping your body, mind, and spirit to flow with healthy energy, instead of stagnate. Approach it with the utmost love for you, and they will feel this in turn and respond however they can.

You are not responsible for how they respond. If you are unkind to them, then you are. If you are expressing your own feelings, then that is all that you are responsible for. You are responsible for getting this energy out of your body, but not for how they take that. This was a huge lesson for me to learn throughout my life. I likely learned it mostly from being a manager in our office. Things needed to be said and done and there was no intention to hurt or anger a person. The goal was always to address what I or my business required. I hurt some of my staff when I spoke and a few were brave enough to voice it, and I thank them for that. I learned from those experiences and how to speak without blame or hurt or by personalizing it. It does take practice.

In the classes I have taught regarding this information, I have challenged those listening to pull out their phones and schedule a time to talk to the person with whom they are having issues. I only have had a few takers. It is uncomfortable, but once you become comfortable expressing your feelings, you will live in an amazing state of ease.

Imagine, for a moment, all the people you would rather walk across the street to avoid rather than face. I have two in my life right now I can think of as I'm writing this. What if you expressed your feelings to them, or just got the feelings out of your body so that they no longer triggered you? What kind of joy and ease would that create for you?

2.   Have a Fake Conversation

Remember, this is all for you and no one else. If a person has passed, or is not willing to meet you, or you are too charged to meet face-to-face, this is the next best thing. Imagine that the person who has triggered you is sitting across the table from you (do this sometime when you are alone). Put duct tape over their mouth - it's your imagination and self-therapy! Then, start talking and don't hold back. Scream, yell, swear, get the emotion out of your body, and tell them how you really feel.

After the initial scream, you may find you are able to have a face-to-face conversation. Once the charge on the matter dissipates for you, you may be more able to express how their words or actions made you feel. Fake conversations feel good, but truthfully, having a live conversation is still the most effective way to resolve issues.

Fake conversations are great if a person has passed away, if there is a group of people, or if you are too explosive to face the person and want to cause bodily harm. Being alone in your vehicle is a fantastic way to have a fake conversation. This is also a good way to practice a face-to-face conversation. Remember, this is all for you and your body, and to ensure that your energy keeps flowing and does not become stuck in the body.

3.   Write, Journal, or Express Yourself Creatively

You may have been told to write or journal your feelings, but why does this really help? This is a form of self-expression, and therefore, it is the same as screaming it out. If you connect to writing, this is for you. You do not have to censor what you are saying. Treat it as self-therapy. This is an expression of who you are. Make no apologies! You may feel compelled to write on social media, but I'd suggest posting to share what you are learning rather than trashing another person.

Besides writing, there are many other ways to create. Painting, sketching, coloring, woodworking, and crafts are all great ways to express yourself. Expressing yourself creatively, especially if it involves using your hands, is a great way to release negative emotions and get energy flowing again.

We are creative beings. This part of our brain is sometimes forgotten and we get stuck in figuring out the logic instead of playing, creating, imagining, or using our intuition. I used to include cooking and baking in this creative expression, but as my friend Marlena pointed out, pouring your anger and frustration into something you will eat is not a great idea.

4.   Talk to a Trusted Friend

Note the word *trusted*. If you have a friend that talks about other people in a gossipy way, they, unfortunately, are not a trusted friend. A trusted friend is someone that has your back and will honour your secrets and life. You may have no one. If you are really fortunate, you may have one or two of these people in your life. We have a lot of acquaintances in the world, but to have a trusted friend is rare.

This is a great lesson for when people are expressing themselves to you. It's not always necessary to give advice. Listening is a gift. You may say to them, "I don't need advice. I just need a listening ear to work through some of my frustration with this certain person." You want the person to hold space for you and just be a sounding board.

As a trusted friend, you may even say, "Do you need me to just listen or would you like my advice?" This approach is powerful because if you just rattled off your advice and tried to fix things, it may not be heard, because it was never requested. Sometimes people just need to vent; you may need that some days too.

5.   Healthy Physical Expression

You can move your body out of the emotion. If you have a conflict at work and have to go into another meeting, take a moment to move your body, shake it, or dance, and the frustrated energy will have a chance to be changed within you. At the very least, take some deep breaths. This changes the energy around you.

Three easy ways to get energy moving in your body include:

- Big Arm Circles: this helps to detach energetic cords
- Scooping Earth Energy: do a few squats and use your arms as the scoop to gather the Earth's energy. Just scoop the air by your ankles and then move the air/energy over your body to replenish what you need.
- Limp Arm Body Twist: this stimulates the kidneys, which are the organs responsible for

removing waste in the body. In traditional Chinese Medicine, it's believed that the kidneys hold the emotion of fear. To release and stimulate new energy flow, allow your hands to gently swing around your body with your hands tapping the back of you and the front of you.

Screaming or yelling into a pillow or in your car also helps. Punching a pillow or throwing rocks (not at others, but maybe into a lake or river) also helps. Drumming is another great way to express yourself. We hear too much about how some people are expressing themselves by either taking a life or through physical abuse. That doesn't contribute to you or others. There are healthier ways.

The important message is to get the energy out of the body so that it does not congest into a physical symptom or condition. More importantly, know you are worthy of peace. You are worthy of ease. You are worthy of joy without conditions, so do this for you!

Thoughts to Ponder:

1. Are there any people in your life who you would be uncomfortable meeting on the street?
2. What can you do today to get the energy you are avoiding or that is triggering you out of your body?

CHAPTER 23

CHAKRA #6 – THE THIRD EYE CHAKRA

The third eye chakra is located in the middle of your forehead between your eyes. It is your sixth sense, your intuition, and it provides insight and a sense of knowing. When this chakra is open and functioning properly, we are able to enter different dimensions. The physical structures involved with this chakra include the eyes, ears, brain, mouth, teeth, nose, and everything from the top of the neck up.

Our senses are a bonus to the body. Have you ever wondered why we have them? When a client comes in stressed and is expecting complete relaxation in just one hour, I often tell them to tune into their senses. When a person only focuses on what they are feeling, hearing, smelling, seeing, and tasting, they have no other place to be but in the present moment. Eckhart Tolle teaches this in his book The Power of Now. When we live in the future, we have a greater chance of anxiety. When we live in the past, we have a greater chance of depression. The only place to live is right here and now. Our mind loves taking us to other places, and our body responds to that. We become anxious focusing on the future, because we cannot live in the future. We are not there; we are only here right now. The now is all we have.

The mind is such a powerful thing. It can take you into complete chaos or into complete relaxation. The body doesn't know the difference between reality (the now) and perceived reality (future or past). It will respond to whatever you focus upon. This little bit of information makes meditation all the more valuable. When I teach meditation, I explain that when we consciously choose to observe the body and mind, we come into the present moment. This is really the only place to live. Nothing else exists or truthfully matters.

It is interesting to note that all the senses are in the sixth chakra plus what we feel throughout our body. When we are completely present in the here and now, we have a greater chance to use our sixth sense, our third eye chakra, because we will be able to sense it. When the mind throws you into chaos (past or future), this sense is not as easy to interpret.

This makes a great case for slowing down and quieting your life, even just for a few moments a day. When you can do this and you start to use your intuition, miracles will start to happen. Once you experience the miracles, you will wonder why you ever shut this chakra down or why you never explored how to open or balance it.

Since I began practicing coming into the present moment, miracles have started to become part of my everyday life. Years ago, I was on a solo retreat in Victoria, BC, Canada. I saw a billboard for a new real estate development that looked interesting. I inquired as to where it was and the price of the units. I was in touch with the developer and kept being updated with what was going on. I put all this information in a folder labeled "Dreams". This condominium development was right by the ocean, had a community garden, yoga studio, coffee shop, professional kitchen, and entertainment area. It felt like home to me.

I told my husband about it and he laughed it off. Somehow that didn't seem to bother me. I just kept dreaming about living there. About 18 months later, my husband and I were exploring retirement options and had checked out a new build in a city a few hours away from where we lived. We were driving home when we both turned to each other and said we didn't want to spend the last of our life in this city. We had lived there before and the winters were still frigid! Craig then asked me about the place in BC that I had told him about a year and a half earlier.

I'm still laughing at how this all played out. I sent him the information, and he got in touch with the developers. To make a long story short, we now have the retirement place that I dreamed about so very long ago!

How I read energy and get messages for myself comes from how I feel. The place in Victoria felt amazing! I could also see us living there very easily. I still don't know when we will permanently move there, but I know with each year it gets closer. I can feel it more than I can hear, see, taste, or smell it. These senses are called your clairs.

- Clairvoyance is a sense of seeing.
- Clairaudience is a sense of hearing.
- Clairsentience is a sense of feeling.
- Clairalience is a sense of smelling.
- Clairgustance is a sense of tasting.
- Claircognizance is a sense of knowing.

I use claircognizance and clairsentience the most. I have my own intuitive strengths, as do you. The more you tap into the way you sense intuition, the stronger your intuitive muscle becomes. Most people are just opening up to the idea that they may be intuitive. If your third eye chakra has remained closed for a long time, it is time to make it shine! Just imagine the ease of life when you have another tool to guide you.

Intuition comes from our right brain. It is developed as a child by being involved in play, creativity, imagination, and daydreaming. Our left brain governs the more logical side of life and manages schedules, data, and structure. We need and use both, but as an adult we use the left side of the brain a lot more. Think of your day today. How much time did you spend playing? Did you have some time to create or daydream? These sound like silly things to do yet these activities all help activate your intuition. Plus, they are a lot more fun!!

If you are looking for ways to open this chakra to enjoy life in a greater capacity, start with scheduling some play time. Kids and pets can help you with this. Grab some friends and play a table game, colour in a colouring book, or sit and daydream with a cup of tea. Spend some time with yourself and get to know this part of you that can truthfully act like a superpower.

When you lead with your intuition and access your higher self, life is very peaceful. You come to have a greater understanding of a larger picture at play. If logic tells you that something is wrong, but your clair is screaming for your attention, wake up and listen to it. Play with it to start its development. Ask for it to show itself to you.

Thoughts to Ponder:

1. Where do you live: past, future, or present?
2. When have you felt your intuition move you?
3. Which clair is the strongest for you?
4. When was the last time you scheduled some play or daydreaming time?

CHAPTER 24

CHAKRA #7 – THE CROWN CHAKRA

The crown chakra is located on the top of the head and just above it. This is your communication line to your Higher Power, God, Universe, Creator or whatever you want to call it.

This chakra is an untapped resource for most people. Much of society does not have a relationship with this part of themselves or the mystical universe. Even most religious people go through the motions of ritual and must-do's, but never really develop the deep connection to spirit that they crave, and quite possibly, don't even know they crave.

This untapped resource is just waiting for us to ask for its assistance. That's the thing - we must ask. Asking is a form of surrender. It's also a form of respect. We surrender to something greater than us, something that possibly coordinates the greater picture of life and is always looking out for us. It is a form of respect to acknowledge this force and to humbly accept its help.

When a person starts the conversation and the relationship with our Higher Self begins, trust follows and true magic starts to take place. Peace that surpasses all understanding is also felt. Here's a quick example:

A couple months ago, I was chilling out on a beach in Maui when I had the idea to hold a group healing session in my business. I played with that energy for a while, and by the time I was flying home, I had it all arranged with registrations coming in. Back home, I sat in the studio just minutes before everyone was to arrive and had a mini panic attack. My thoughts raced. "What am I doing? This is silly! I don't know how to do this. I don't even know what to do!"

I sat with this for a while and then heard, "You, Cari, are doing nothing. Relax. Your work is done." I wondered about that for a moment, and then decided to trust this little voice, because it has never let me down.

The class participants began to arrive, and I used my breath to calm down my anxious ego. As it turned out, the evening and series went amazingly well! There were major spiritual breakthroughs for almost everyone who came. I got out of my own way and just let spirit take over. For anyone who has never done this, I was tuning into my clairs and following what I was feeling and knowing. There were techniques I did that I had never done before. I trusted the messages that I was getting. It was so much fun for me. Still, each time the group met, I struggled with those ego thoughts, but overrode them with trust.

Gabrielle Bernstein says, "The Universe always has your back." Being a woman who chose to not have children, I struggled to understand unconditional love. I understood this love once I got my fur babies (my cats). I thought kids and pets were the only way to this understanding. It turns out I was overlooking two important things that also have our back and love us unconditionally: 1. Our bodies. Yes, they do and they do many things each minute to protect us and help us function. 2. The Universe, God, Creator or whatever you want to call 'It'.

You may ask, "What about all the bad stuff that happens in the world? Does God have our backs then?" I believe we have to dig a bit deeper. I'll share my thoughts, but, in all honesty, you have to find your own truth with this as with everything in life. I believe we are infinite, meaning we cannot die. Sure, our body dies and I believe it dies over and over but your spirit, your soul, moves from lifetime to lifetime. It has experiences that will have you continually learning, growing, and helping mankind.

When something tragic happens, there is a greater picture involved than what we can sometimes understand as a human. I'm sure you have heard some stories that will support my statements, but I would like to give you one of my own.

In 1998, my husband at the time told me he wanted a divorce. I was crushed. He was my first true love, and I thought we would be together forever. My world went crazy. I remember thinking I was mentally ill and that I needed the help of a counsellor to get me through it. I did. My counsellor not only got me through the rough days of separation, but also helped me find my true self. It was with her guidance that I am who I am today. Without that help, I would not have found my own truth about life, and would have continued to follow the crowd hiding the person who I came here to be! I have told my ex-husband that I am so thankful that we married and got divorced, because it helped me find ME. It was my live 'near death experience', and I can now say (and it took a good 10 years) that this experience was the best thing that has ever happened to me.

There are many uglier things that happen such as abuse and death that when dissected deeply, you can find the spiritual 'aha moment'. If you look at tragedy through human eyes, you may never see the beauty. If you look at it through the crown chakra, you can find the glory of all the pains of life.

Thoughts to Ponder:

1. How is your relationship with your Higher Self?

2. What do you call your Higher Self?

3. When is the last time you trusted this force within?

4. Have any of your own tragedies turned to triumphs within your spirit?

CHAPTER 25

RESTORING THE BODY

I didn't really understand the importance of body/mind/spirit restoration until well into my massage career. Stressed out people, mostly women, were drawn to my practice to just relax and receive. I grew up in a generation where the word lazy was used when we sat still or were not running from event to event. This word was passed down through our ancestors. If you think about your grandparents' lives, they did not have the luxury of watching TV, binging on Netflix, or having a bubble bath. Our kids' generation today has perhaps gone to the other side of the spectrum, though I'm sure it will balance out one day.

Taking a break from life should not just happen on the

weekends and the few weeks of holidays you may receive during the year. Relaxation should be a part of every day. Have you ever travelled to Spain? Isn't it frustrating trying to go shopping when the stores are closed after lunch? This is their siesta time or their time to rest. Could you imagine the productivity of North Americans if we had a siesta after a leisurely lunch (which always included wine)?

This same relaxing application should be taken into consideration after a huge life event, such as a death, divorce, nursing someone back to health, extended help to a loved one, abuse, or a major health issue. We should place enough value on our lives to take the time to rest and restore after these crises. I remember meeting a dear soul, who has since passed, one day in my office. She had just been looking after her mom who passed away in her care. This client was exhausted physically and emotionally. We agreed she needed some time to restore so that her body, mind, and spirit could come back to life. We started to make a plan for her that included weekly massage and daily extreme self-care. Eventually, she began to find her new normal after a loss. This advice has remained true and effective for many clients who came after her.

Another client of mine was just the opposite. His parents passed, he retired, and he has been to numerous friends' funerals; yet, he continues to push through life as though nothing has phased him. I recognize that everyone processes things differently. I also observe that his body is broken, his mind is confused, and there is nothing in his life that he does for his soul. He finds things to keep him busy, likely so that he doesn't have to feel. Although I honour that, I believe there is another way to move through hardship. Taking the time to process change as well as physical and emotional pain can allow one to move through life more freely.

I read an interesting story by Atherton Drenth. She is the author of The Intuitive Dance, a beautiful book that contains many tips for life. She writes about a cat and dog encounter and how animals know when it is time to rest and restore. Here is my interpretation of this story:

Once upon a time there was a cat named Fluffy who loved to explore the outdoors - so many smells to experience and birds to catch. As Fluffy was sniffing his way through the garden, he came upon a rather large dog that had escaped his owner's leash. They met each other face-to-face, and Fluffy, being quite a bit smaller than the dog, needed to make a decision - should he run or should he fight? Knowing that the chances of survival were greater if he ran, he ran. The chase was on. Both animals experienced an increase in adrenalin. Blood flowed quicker through their bodies making it easier to react. Their pupils dilated to allow more focus. Both bodies were moving fast. The dog's teeth were close to the cat as he was barking and running. The dog grabs Fluffy and flings him across the yard. The cat lands on its feet and keeps running. A tree saves Fluffy. Up he climbs, while the dog is stuck below barking and growling. After some time, the dog finally gives up and leaves, distracted by something else that caught its attention. The cat doesn't immediately come down and continue on with life. Fluffy knows to rest. He licks his wounds and stays up in the tree until all the physiological signs of the fight or flight response disappear.

I'm sure you have heard of the flight or fight response. It works the same in humans. Our pupils dilate, our heart rate increases, blood flow moves to the limbs, and adrenalin and cortisol are released to give the body a super burst of energy. These are built-in amazing responses for when we are threatened. Fluffy understands that these responses are activated within his body and waits until his body returns to normal before proceeding.

Many humans keep on going after a threat to their well-being without taking the proper time to rest and restore. We are smart sometimes, aren't we? When we keep going and other stressors appear in life, we handle it in the same way, but the response (fight or flight) is never turned off if the stressors keep appearing. When the fight or flight response is continually being activated, smaller stressors such as spilled coffee on your shirt are treated as a major crisis. The body then responds as if a buffalo is chasing it (something our ancestors may have experienced).

There are many people who have trouble sleeping at night or who are irritable when anything happens that has not been planned. Is it possible that your body is always perceiving it is being attacked, chased, or under stress? Has your fight or flight physiological response ever shut off? Have you allowed for your body to rest after a stressful event?

How does one rest? This is something that is never taught to us, especially by our family who considers rest to be lazy. Taking extreme care of yourself during and after stress is one of the kindest things you can do for yourself.

What brings you rest? What helps you to chill out? Do you even know? When was the last time you felt rested? If you know what helps you rest and restore, then, that is what you should do. Here are some of the ways I relax: sitting on the couch petting my cat, enjoying a salt bath, receiving a massage, listening to music, going for a walk, doing yoga, playing my piano, having light conversation, or watching a comedy. I do not get involved in a project or busyness of any kind. It's all about nurturing me and being selfish because I (and YOU) am worth it! I may take time off work or slow the schedule down. I will eat and drink what my body wants and sleep without guilt whenever my body needs. Again, if you know what will nourish you, that is what you do. Sometimes you may need to escape to a cabin in the forest or to your favourite hotel or resort.

One of my favourite getaways is in British Columbia, Canada. I have ventured to this resort all by myself and booked a room overlooking the ocean. I would open the patio and light the fire and just sit, journal, or colour. I would go for a walk or swim in the outdoor pool while it rained. I would drink wine in the bubble bath. I would always indulge in at least one spa treatment and try new things on the menu. I also enjoyed just sitting and watching people. Getting away is very restorative to my body, mind, and spirit.

Find your own way. Find a way that will help you through the stress in life. The world still needs you fully. Please take the time to restore your body, mind, and spirit, especially after a huge life event.

Thoughts to Ponder:

1. What are your family's thoughts on rest? Are they yours also or do you think differently?
2. Is your body currently under the fight or flight response?
3. What brings nourishment to your body, mind, and spirit?
4. What can you do today to rest? Do you need a major break or even just a little one?

CHAPTER 26

COLLECTIVE CONSCIOUSNESS

Collective consciousness may be a new thought to many people. Yet, others are very familiar with the power of it and the meaning of it for their life. To me, it's a fairly new thought, but one I can't deny anymore. I have been very unaware of the thought of connectedness and togetherness for most of my life.

The first time I became aware of collective consciousness was from a tragic event that happened in my hometown. A few years ago, we woke up to the news of a double murder of a family that I had never met. This literally shocked our community of less than 6000 people. More interestingly was that there was a mourning felt for this family from everyone in our community, even from those who had never met them.

Everyone somehow had a connection to their kids, family, or neighbours. It felt like the whole town was mourning. The energy was very thick and heavy. I shed tears for them, even though I wasn't even sure what they looked like.

Is it possible for me to be sad for people I don't even know? Yes! It is! This is tuning into the collective. It's feeling what is going on in the hearts of others. I was connecting to the pulse of what was happening around me and being conscious of it.

An interesting situation happened with a family member last year that also showed me how collective consciousness works. Most summers in my wellness centre, there is always a slight drop off in business, because people go to the lake for their vacation. We live in the beautiful boreal forest surrounded by fresh water lakes where people enjoy camping, fishing, swimming, and hiking. One day, a family member was in for a visit and he said he was going to hold off booking his next appointment because he was going to spend some time at the lake. I nearly fell off my chair, because he doesn't even like the lake. We have to beg him to come out and spend time at the cabin. In fact, the year that he said this, he only was at the lake four times, and only for supper. He never spent the night.

He had said needing to be at the lake would get in the

way of scheduling his next appointment; yet, it wasn't true. He didn't know that every other person that week was planning to be at the lake. How did that energy, that collective conscious thought, get inside his brain? He was aware of the collective. Can you imagine what else we may go around thinking to be our truth when we are just affected by collective consciousness?

Another example of collective consciousness was when a semi truck hit the Humboldt Broncos hockey team bus and 16 people, mostly hockey players, died. Humboldt, Saskatchewan, Canada is 400 kilometers from our town and most people in our community did not know these kids, yet we mourned them. The world mourned them. The world didn't know what to do with their mourning and raised the most money ever collected on a GoFundMe page. That is collective consciousness mourning. It was horrible to keep watching this on the news and Facebook feeds, but it was beautiful to see how people were coming together and supporting the families involved. We need even more of this consciousness in the world, not just for a hockey team, but for all the tragedy that appears around us.

Can we be collectively conscious of the good happening around us? Why is it that tragedy brings us together? Why do we not celebrate and support one another even when there is no pain or suffering? What would this even look like?

A different example of collective consciousness that I believe has an effect on our planet is the weather. You may live in an area where people have more to talk about than the weather. In my town, for the farmers and retirees, this is possibly their favourite go-to conversation starter. Do you think it's possible when multiple people are commenting on how windy (insert whatever is the daily complaint) it is that the universe responds by giving us more wind?

My last observation of the power of collective consciousness is at huge music festivals. Music holds another element of vibration. Have you ever been at a concert with thousands of people and just started crying for no real reason other than being moved? I admit I have, many times. The power of the collective consciousness loving something in common feels too overwhelming to not respond. Even if you do not like concerts or have never experienced this, I encourage you to google "Green Day Crowd Singing Bohemian Rhapsody" and watch the video. A crowd of 60,000 people sing Bohemian Rhapsody together before a Green Day concert starts. Green Day was just playing some background tracks prior to their concert when the crowd breaks out in song. The feeling is incredible and undeniable. That is a powerful example of how music brings people together and unites our consciousness.

We must realize that we contribute to the creative power of the collective consciousness. When you think, "Oh how awful; how tragic; how horrible!", what you are feeling is created, especially if there are thousands, tens of thousands, or millions of people doing it. This makes a case for limiting your news watching and reading on all platforms. If we are in this constant state of horror, what does that really do to the world around us both personally and collectively?

We could have a more positive effect if we thought together, "Oh how amazing, how beautiful, and how peaceful." World meditation sits have strived for a more positive collective response in mankind. With social media and technology making it much easier to live and think as one, why not use this to increase our consciousness collectively to enhance all of our well-being?

These are things to ponder. See what resonates with your own truth. How can you use this knowledge to change some things in your world for the better? There will likely never be a double-blind study to prove or disprove any of these collective conscious thoughts. You must find your own truth and maybe these questions and the ones in the previous chapters will lead you down your own path to experience life in a greater way.

Thoughts to Ponder:

1.   Have you experienced collective consciousness?

2. What part did you play in it?
3. Do you have ideas to help humankind enhance collective consciousness for something other than tragedy?
4. How can you make that happen?

CONCLUSION

B y the observations and life experiences I have seen and lived, I hope you, too, can see the importance of paying attention to the energy in and around your body, home, work space, and world. Once you acknowledge energy, and experience it first hand, it becomes a part of you. Energy is a part of you, but most of us are not aware or conscious of it. By bringing this awareness into your life, you will activate it.

Energy is everywhere, in all things, and it is all things. That includes you! You are energy! Would it not make sense to learn more about this wonderful world of energy, and use it to empower your life?

Energy is like our untapped superpower. It's time to be the superhero of your own life. Find your truth and what resonates for you in your world. My hope for you is that you are able to become conscious of the energetic changes and connections that are just waiting for you to experience and enjoy, so that your life begins to flow with more ease and peace.

RESOURCES TO HELP YOU ON YOUR JOURNEY

www.mindvalley.com

Anatomy of the Spirit – Caroline Myss

Energy Medicine – Donna Eden with David Feinstein, Ph.D.

Energy Medicine – C. Norman Shealy, MD, Ph.D.

Molecules of Emotion – Candace B. Pert, Ph.D.

The Field – Lynne McTaggart

The Intuitive Dance – Atherton Drenth

The Power of Now – Eckhart Tolle

ABOUT THE AUTHOR

Cari Moffet is a Registered Massage Therapist, Life Coach, Meditation Teacher, Reiki Master, and Certified Medical Intuitive. She is an expert at reducing stress in her clients. She uses her many gifts and talents to relax and recharge a client's mind, body, and spirit to health and wholeness. Cari has been in the alternative health field since 1996 and she loves guiding people to make choices to enhance their well-being in a natural way.

Cari is also the owner and founder of the award-winning business Wholelife Wellness. She has been featured on Voice America Talk Radio, and has published numerous magazine articles. She also facilitates retreats across North America.

When not at *work* (italicized because most times it seems like play to her), Cari enjoys spending time with her family and friends, playing piano, pottery, reading, and paddling her kayak on the northern Saskatchewan lakes. Most of all, she loves to travel.

Cari resides in Meadow Lake, Saskatchewan, Canada with her husband Craig, her two fur balls (or what some call cats), Fenway and Wrigley.

To find out more about Cari and her work, to book a distant session, or to have her facilitate a class in your area, visit www.carimoffet.com.

Facebook   www.facebook.com/carimoffetintuition
Instagram   www.instagram.com/carimoffet

Made in the USA
Lexington, KY
16 November 2019